Heaven and *Earth*

Other Books by the same author

Life in the World Unseen
More about Life in the World Unseen
Here and Hereafter (originally 'ABC of Life')
Facts
More Light

Heaven and Earth

– more spirit communications
from
Monsignor Robert Hugh Benson

Received & Recorded by

Anthony Borgia

First published 1948
This edition 2020

Published by
Saturday Night Press Publications
England

snppbooks@gmail.com
www.snppbooks.com

ISBN 978-1-908421-43-2

www.snppbooks.com

Cover design: *Ann Harrison (SNPP) with permission to use a
painting of 'Tween Heaven & Earth' by Marjorie Hesford.*

About Anthony Borgia

Anthony Borgia was a fine medium with a strong gift of clairaudience and frequently automatic writing, when he would often feel the weight and warmth of the spirit communicator's hand on his own, guiding the pencil across the paper. It was through these particular aspects of his mediumship that he was able to assist Monsignor Robert Hugh Benson in realising his dearest wish: that of putting into print the knowledge and facts of life after death, and helping to banish the fear of death, which affects so many people.

At the beginning of WW2, he began to sit with Mollie Duncan, the good, non-professional trance-medium in whose circle he was to be a member for 25 years. Here he witnessed Monsignor's first appearance at a séance.

He told a friend: "Mollie's mediumship was of the highest standard. Shortly after the outbreak of war, a new spirit visitor took control at one of the circles. To our astonishment, we saw it was Monsignor. The way he sat, the distinctive tilt of the head with chin up, all revealed the living personality we knew as Monsignor Benson. It was one of the most remarkable first attempts at controlling I have seen... Monsignor spoke clearly and firmly, greeting us as though he was there in his own physical body. At another circle shortly after, he broached the subject of writing: would I undertake it? I raised objections, saying the war had started, paper was getting scarce, I was unknown, and so forth, but he brushed this aside saying that if I would do the job, 'they' would do the rest?"

"Later he referred to something of the organisation which had gone into bringing the books about, telling us that the entire process had begun many years before, and he had been under the guidance of spirit beings from far higher spheres than his own. None of them would have permitted him to say anything which was not true, even in the unlikely event he wished to do so."

When Anthony was writing the books, he was anxious that the accuracy of the scripts should have independent verification, insofar as this was possible. At the weekly trance circle, he would always check with Monsignor that every word had been 'heard and transcribed' accurately.

Anthony passed in 1989 at the age of 93, a man of profound intelligence allied to an enquiring mind, whose interests were many and varied, although those which remained the strongest and lasted all his life were the study of music and of psychic science, in both of which he could be considered something of an expert. A man of great kindness, warmth and generosity, he was a splendid example of true Spiritualism, never exhibiting this better than during the many years of near-blindness in his old age when the grace, courage and humour with which he bore this affliction drew the admiration of all who knew him.

The books for which Anthony acted as Monsignor's amanuensis are rightly regarded as among the 'classics' of Spiritualist literature. It was always a source of great happiness to him that he had helped, in this way, to spread the great truths of Spiritualist teachings. His books remain as a testimony to Monsignor's great desire to share his knowledge of the life to come, and to Anthony's own homage to Truths which sustained him throughout his long life.

Contents

My Home Enlarged

So many of my reader friends, being painfully conscious of the immense and disruptive changes that have taken place upon earth, have been led to ponder what changes, if any at all, have occurred in the spirit world.

They know that neither we nor the lands wherein we live are static, that we are forever progressing and advancing, and that while we cannot undergo the vast upheavals that have so violently shaken and disturbed the earth world, bringing havoc and ruin, yet things must have altered with us in some measure, in some manner, since that time when I first 'broke the silence of the grave' in these writings.

Incidentally, what a dismal, melancholy phrase is that: to break the silence of the grave! How can the silence of any grave be broken? That which lies in the tomb is but lifeless matter. I—the *real* I—was at no time in any grave. However, let us think of something more cheerful and pleasant than graves.

My friends, too, are very kindly interested in my own welfare, and they wonder how I have 'got on' during these passing years of your calendar.

The first question we will discuss later. For the present, in answer to the many friendly thoughts that have come to me, I can say that I am truly well, happy, and supremely contented. Of personal changes there has been none worthy of your interest. I am fully occupied, managing to make myself useful in a number of directions.

You will doubtless recall that among my various activities is that of helping folk when they are making their entrance into these lands at their 'death'. I work in company with others, chief among whom are my two old friends, Edwin and Ruth. The former, you will also recollect, is an erstwhile priestly colleague of my earthly days who met me upon my arrival here, and whose welcome presence I was overjoyed to have in those initial moments immediately following upon my transition.

Ruth is a young lady of great charms whom we met upon my journeying forth, under Edwin's able guidance, to see the wonders of these lands. She joined our expedition, upon our invitation, with great alacrity as she was in similar case to myself. That is, she was a new arrival, and was just as ignorant of everything concerning this glorious new life as I was.

From that moment of our first encounter we have been fast friends. The three of us work closely together, so closely, in fact, that both Edwin and Ruth spend far more time in my home than they do in their own. A most happy and pleasant arrangement. Beautiful is Ruth's own dwelling yet there is something that appeals to her in the old house which has been my home since my advent into these realms.

There is nothing very outstanding about this house, though it is incomparably more beautiful now than its counterpart in which I lived when on earth. But it suits my purpose. Indeed, I can say it suits the purpose of all three of us. I have mentioned the house to you before and given you one or two details concerning it so that I will not make myself tedious by going over old ground. I must tell you that Ruth has undertaken the entire disposition of it in all matters, and I am perfectly content to leave it so.

Though there may be no observable changes in myself, we have, however, made an addition to the house. It came about in this way. First, I must explain that there are thousands of people engaged upon work similar to our own. We are really all part of one organisation, but we work in small groups. Edwin sometimes undertakes—we all do at times in more or less degree—some task alone as on the occasion when he met me at my dissolution.

But we find by experience that when we come forward to offer our help to people who have just left the earth at their 'death', and who, knowing nothing of the true state of life here, fervently and fearfully believe that they are to be dragged off to a frightful Judgement, we find in such cases that the force of our numbers adds weight to our words as we each individually explain to the sorely perplexed soul that there is nothing to fear, nothing to cause the least anxiety. That soul can turn from one to another of us, three different personalities, different in feature and form, real and human in appearance and voice, and he can seek corroboration—and find it.

We present nothing of an angelic appearance that would, in good truth, terrify the new arrival out of his wits, and serve to conjure up images in his mind of 'the angel of death'—whoever that may be. I have been present at many passings, but I have not yet encountered this peculiar being. He is just one of the strange adjuncts so closely associated in the minds of some folk with 'the awful change', as the simple procedure of passing into the spirit world has been so stupidly denominated.

Our purpose is to calm any fears and induce

tranquillity of mind so that everything is eliminated or avoided that would tend to obstruct our efforts and add to our labours. When Edwin met me, he was in clerical attire, exactly as I remembered him, and I was similarly habited. Now Edwin normally wears his spirit habiliments when he is in his own realm, but if he had met me clothed in such manner, then just as surely should I have taken fright—of that I am convinced. But to see him standing there looking precisely as he did of old when on earth, together with his cheerful countenance, at once served to reassure me. And that saved Edwin a vast deal of labour.

Although the women-folk, of course, are fully represented among us, by far the larger part of our particular section of this organisation consists of men who were clergymen during their earthly lives.

Transitions vary so greatly in their circumstances that we find it to be of first rate advantage if we meet, fairly frequently, all those who are connected with our own group, to discuss our individual experiences and to exchange and compare notes. It increases our knowledge prodigiously, and provides us with invaluable information upon which we can base any future action of our own when similar circumstances present themselves. Such meetings take place over a wide area of these realms—it is not an original and exclusive idea of our own! Our meeting-place varies as we each take it in turn to act as host or chairman to our companions, just as so many small society meetings are conducted upon earth.

When it devolved upon me to accommodate our friends, hitherto we had always met in a chamber upon the upstairs floor of my house. The chamber that was set apart for these gatherings is extremely pleasant, but hardly large enough for convenience and comfort.

It is true, the view from this upper floor is enchanting, but then we do not forgather merely to gaze upon the undoubted splendour of the scene.

As the numbers of our workers grew, I felt the time had come to provide other and more adequate accommodation. Edwin and Ruth, who had naturally perceived the state of affairs as readily as I had done, were in hearty agreement with me. We thereupon betook ourselves outside into the gardens to survey our little domain, and at length we decided upon the right spot upon which to build an extension or annexe to the main building. We discussed the style and form the new room should take, its interior and exterior disposition, how it should be furnished, and such details of like nature.

The first active step thereafter was to consult the ruler of the realm, lay our proposals and plans before him, and seek his approval. For though we may have earned for ourselves the right to increase the dimensions of our home, that is not to say that we have become a 'law unto ourselves'. For you must know that in these lands everything is done conformably and in good order.

It may puzzle some of my friends as to how we know when we have earned the right to possess anything in particular, which in this instance happens to be an increase in the size of my home. That is a question one finds very difficult to answer. Nor am I alone in this.

So many processes and procedures become as second nature to us here in the course of our lives that we scarcely stop to ponder just when this condition first exerted itself, so to speak, and became part of our lives. Some things, of course, are very apparent. For instance, the first occasion upon which Ruth and I made the attempt to move ourselves by the thought process instead of using our legs in the old method of locomotion, which we had employed hitherto. That we shall never forget. It was such a revolutionary event in our lives.

I fancy that there are not many of us who will forget an experience of that nature for it made us realise very early the immense power of our minds. The most I can say, then, with regard to our absolute knowledge that we are free to possess some particular thing or another, whatever it may be, is that we are conscious that we lack that object, and that we have a strong, deep desire for it. Then we are aware that our desire has passed out from our minds, and in place of the desire there is the unmistakable certainty that we are at liberty to possess. So that the procedure comes to this: first one has the desire to possess, and that thought leaves us. Whence it goes, I am unable to say.

If, after the wish to possess has been projected from our minds, we are entitled to possess, the desire will no longer be as a yearning for in its place will come the knowledge that nothing debars us from becoming owners of what we want. We are, *ipso facto*, virtual possessors. We have then only to take the necessary steps towards actual ownership.

But if we have not yet earned the right to possess then the desire will *remain* with us an *unfulfilled* desire until such time as we have advanced spiritually. We shall be aware of a positive barrier.

In saying that a *knowledge* of the right to possess takes the place of the former *desire* to possess, I would not have you understand that our interest wanes. That is not so. Our interest, in good truth, actually increases. But there is a vast difference between a desire that is only a desire and which must remain as unfulfilled, and a desire that can be transformed into an immediate fulfilment. Your own unhappy experiences during an earthly life will speak with sufficient eloquence upon that point!

This is, I am afraid, a very unsatisfactory account of a very natural process in these lands, but you will understand that there are so many matters upon which we are as yet uninformed. When such is the case, and I cannot give you reasons or explanations of some one process or another, then the best I can do at the moment is to describe what takes place and leave the question of how it takes place either to some expert in these matters or until such occasion when I am a great deal more advanced upon the road of such specialised knowledge.

There are numerous subjects upon which my good friends of earth would like more information, I am fully persuaded, but they will be the first to acknowledge that there are also many questions which are so easy to ask, but more than difficult to answer. Alternatively, there are a deal of questions whose answers would leave you no wiser, not that your intelligence is limited, but because there is much more to be learned and disclosed first. That is precisely the case with your friend who is setting down these words for you, for I must first be able to understand what I am talking about before I can ever hope to frame it in terms sufficiently perspicuous for your own comprehension.

In these varied writings which I have set before you, I have ever aimed at being as clear and precise as it is humanly possible: to shun as you are advised to shun that strange and elusive gentleman, the devil, any account, of whatever nature, that is vague in meaning. The friends who advise me here upon these writings have given me a sound maxim: stick to facts, they say, and leave the trimmings alone.

To return to the new wing of my home. Before setting out to see the ruler of the realm we made, in a roughly drawn sketch, a plan of the new chamber as we should like it to be. We are not accomplished draughtsmen by any means, but we managed to produce a drawing, rather crude, but we hoped sufficiently clear, to place before the ruler, and from which it would be possible for an architect to glean a good understanding of our requirements. We sent forth a message to the ruler explaining our needs, and within a moment's space of time back came the answer, an answer which said, not that he would 'grant us an interview' or that we might 'present ourselves to him' but simply that he *would be most happy to see us.*

There, I think, you have in a few words the true character of this great personage. For he is not a remote and unapproachable being, surrounded by so many satellites that to come within measurable distance of his very presence would be almost an impossibility, except to those who are themselves already illustrious.

Perhaps I shall be challenged upon the quickness of the response made to our request, in that, with such vast numbers of dwellers in these realms, it would be literally out of the question for one man to give interviews to everyone who asked for them without the passage of some considerable time. as you would reckon things on earth. But the fact is precisely as I have stated it to you.

We waited but the instant for our message to travel to the ruler and for his reply to travel back to us. Nor can any degree of privilege whatever be claimed for us in this case. The simple truth is that the ruler is never unnecessarily communicated with in this way unless the need is imperative or otherwise unavoidable. If we can gain what help we need elsewhere, we always do so, but in the matter of erecting a new building of any kind here the ruler is always consulted first. It is a precept from which we never deviate, though conceivably the heavens would not descend if we did.

The most that would happen is that we should have committed a breach of good manners, and taken upon ourselves a high degree of presumption. Our feelings in the circumstances, however, would be sufficient reprimand. No finger would be pointed at us, no word spoken. Our own thoughts would be sufficient. Not only in such cases I am mentioning now would we feel thus, but in any other departure from good taste and the established order of things here.

With our free invitation to call upon the ruler, we set out in great good cheer, for this was something of an event for us. We had oft-times witnessed buildings 'going-up' in different parts of the realm, but this was the first occasion upon which we were actively concerned in the erection of a building that was to be our own.

The ruler himself lives in a most beautiful residence. I would like here to observe that I call him 'ruler' for want of a better term. One might call him 'chief' or 'head' or 'leader' of these realms and yet none would adequately convey the true meaning of the office which he holds. I use the title ruler, therefore, with such reservation as I have made.

We know him here by his personal name. His position and functions being known and understood by everyone, the mere mention of his name is all that is required. We address him by that name. His functions are wide and varied, as you can well imagine, since he acts as a father to us all, rather than as one 'set in authority' over us. *Servus servorum Dei*, he would say in good truth, without affectation, and within the real meaning of that phrase.

The building which he occupies is large since he retains the services of many assistants and colleagues. There is no shortage of willing workers and there is always something to do. The result is efficiency of the highest order in all concerns affecting the welfare of the realm and its inhabitants. He has experts without number upon every branch of human endeavour in these lands.

Those who work for him—and in working for him they are, of course, working for themselves towards greater spiritual progression and advancement—those who work for him are thoroughly conversant with the whole organisation of this realm, each in his own department. The ruler leaves his people to do their work without troublesome interference, knowing that he can rely upon their knowledge, kindliness and good sense. This leaves him free to perform those many little (as he would call them) acts of kindness and helpfulness which have gained him the devoted affection of every dweller in these realms. For it is common to see him upon his way through the lands, enjoying the beauties of the countryside, and being greeted and welcomed upon every hand wheresoever he goes.

Thus we went to seek this great soul. His apartments, in the spacious residence he occupies, are modest and unpretentious; beautifully equipped, it is true, but without those adjuncts with which one might suppose a great leader would be surrounded. In fact, one would describe his 'office' and personal apartments as being decidedly 'homely'. We had but a moment to wait before we were taken to see our friend, and such is the way of things here, we were 'treated like royalty' during that brief while.

As soon as we entered the ruler's chamber he made us heartily welcome, and seated us in comfortable chairs. He knew the purpose of our visit, but none the less, he asked us to give him all the details of our wishes, which he did from motives of pure interest, and not of lordly patronage. There was no question of going 'hat in hand' to use a familiar expression.

He was delighted with our plans and notions for the contemplated extension, made one or two capital suggestions far and away beyond what we had planned, and finally gave the whole scheme his warm-hearted approbation and blessing. With this matter settled so expeditiously, he next enquired about our respective activities, apart from those in which the three of us are concerned together, and then reverting to the purpose of our present visit he invited us to see a man in whom he was much interested, an architect of great skill and originality who, he knew, would be delighted to draw up a proper plan and undertake arrangements for the building itself.

A brief walk brought us to a charming house encircled with tastefully laid-out gardens, through which a pleasant brook ran its clear course. The occupant was seated without doors; he rose upon sight of us, and came forward to greet us. The ruler, of course, he knew at once. A brief introduction, not to make us formally known to our new friend but rather to give him our names, together with such few personal details as would establish a cordial relationship. Had we been strangers entirely upon our own, we should have received just as warm a welcome so that such formalities as were now observed were purely nominal.

Our new friend was geniality itself. He was profuse in his thanks to the ruler when the latter had explained the reason for our descent upon him in such numbers. He was happy to do all he could, and as, he said, he was at the moment merely idling away his time, we could go into our business at once. We were amused at his description of his present situation as we had only a moment since been told by the ruler that he was a most industrious soul who never seemed to stop work for an instant.

The architect took us into his workroom, and we seated ourselves round a table upon which were large sheets of paper and a variety of drawing instruments. Rather diffidently I drew out our crude sketch, which certainly appeared more like a child's scrawl in the presence of so many skilfully drawn plans and designs, which we could perceive in different parts of the room. He laughed at our hesitancy and complimented us by telling us that on many occasions he did not have even the roughest scratchings on paper, and relied upon what he knew his enquirer wanted.

Fortunately for many of us similarly situated, it is not at all necessary to make elaborate plans, provided we know in our minds what it is we want. If we have some moderately clear conception of our needs, the perceptive faculties of the architects of these and other realms can quickly ascertain exactly what is required. That, of course, applies to all of us here. The experts in the numerous crafts will soon gather what we desire, and in most instances will make capital suggestions of which one never dreamt. A final and complete plan is made, however, for the masons, and that our friendly architect now proceeded to do.

The new chamber was to be longer than it was broad, and rectangular; a sort of 'great hall' upon a smaller scale. There would be windows upon three sides, and double doors at each end, one pair of which would afford entrance from the main building, and the farther pair would lead directly into the gardens so that whichever way we happened to glance we should see the trees and the flowers and the lawns beyond.

The windows themselves were to be mullioned, with some coloured glass introduced at the top. The question of panelling arose, and we were a little undecided upon this point. Just then Ruth turned to the architect and whispered something to him. As the ruler, who had remained with us, and Edwin and I were obviously not meant to hear, we became studiously occupied with our own conversation. But we could not help an occasional glance at the two of them. There was evidently some little secret in progress. We observed the architect point to a series of positions upon the plan he was making. Ruth smiled and nodded whereupon the architect smiled and nodded too. He had seemingly joined the conspiracy as well.

At length the plan was sufficiently advanced for us to see how the new chamber would look, and we could but admire the general prospect with the additions which the ruler had made, together with those which the architect had himself introduced. There was to be no delay in the proceedings and after we had made another call, this time to the hall of fabrics, and thence returned home, we should find everyone there assembled to commence operations.

As the architect would himself be present to witness his work being created, we bade him brief good-bye, and walked to the hall of fabric. Here we chose a choice carpet for the floor, a beautiful piece of work, thick in texture and rich in colour, to tread upon the pile of which was like walking upon a finely kept lawn. We arranged for what furniture we needed, and at length arrived at our home.

Of details of the actual erection, it should not be necessary for me to speak, for elsewhere I have given a fairly close account of how buildings are set up in these lands. The method is the same in all cases, and the present one is no exception. It was vastly interesting, however, and as Ruth firmly declared, positively thrilling, to watch our own new apartment growing into life before our eyes. Our enthusiasm was shared by many other folk, and we were the recipients of a host of complimentary remarks, just as on numerous occasions we had complimented others in like circumstances.

Before the work actually commenced the ground had been prepared. That is to say, as we were to build upon a site that was already carefully laid out in lawns and flowerbeds, the latter were removed into other quarters so that nothing was lost. Once the requisite space was clear, then work began, and so soon as the main structure was created the few adornments that we had decided upon were added.

For instance, the insertion of the stained glass in the windows. At length the whole chamber was completed, and we were invited to step within and inspect it. With a word of invitation to the assembly of friends and neighbours who had gathered to watch the proceedings, we entered. Ruth, Edwin, and I were enchanted with the absolute perfection of the work, and we expressed our gratitude to both the ruler and the architect for their respective suggestions which, indeed, crowned the work.

At present the chamber was without furniture, and completely bare. I bethought myself of one or two pieces that were to be found in different parts of the house, and which I had collected from time to time. They had been beautifully carved by skilled craftsmen, and I thought they would suit our new room admirably. With this idea in mind, I left my companions for a moment to seek out the several articles—a cabinet, chairs, and so on.

It was a little while before I returned. When I did so, it was to find that the carpet we had chosen had been laid, and a long and very substantial-looking table had been placed down the centre of the chamber with a number of chairs round it, and notably a fine, heavily carved armchair at the head of it.

Possibly my friends had put it into my head to leave the new apartment on my quest. Whatever was the truth—and I have my suspicions—imagine my surprise and delight when I observed, hanging upon the walls between the windows, six of the most exquisite tapestries. This, I learned, was the outcome of the whispered conspiracy carried on between Ruth and the architect when we had discussed whether or not we should panel the wall. It appeared that Ruth had made these hangings herself and had kept them by her, awaiting suitable opportunity for their disposal. The moment had at last come, she said, when they would be put to a good use.

The tapestries depicted rural scenes, showing an abundance of flowers and trees, and they had been so fashioned that when the whole six of them were hung in close juxtaposition, they formed a long and continuous panorama of countryside. But each could be used separately and apart if desired and still form a complete picture in itself, as they were more or less at present, since they were hung between each of the windows.

When Ruth had first come to these lands she had studied the art of tapestry weaving as a profitable occupation and pleasant amusement, and here were hanging the fruits, or some of them at least, of her industry. My friends will doubtless have in mind the kind of tapestries common upon earth, with their rather dull olive greens and browns, altogether exhibiting something of a faded look, pleasant enough as suggesting other days and the effect of time upon the fabric.

But tapestries of the spirit world are very different. The colours are bright and fresh, clear and glowing, but without being garish. The colours of nature are accurately and minutely reproduced. As we stood gazing upon Ruth's clever handiwork, one could almost forget that we were looking upon woven material, or indeed material of any kind. It seemed as though the walls had disappeared and that we were viewing the actual countryside.

As the light came through the stained glass at the upper sections of the windows, the whole chamber was bathed in the most exquisite tints and blends of colour. Here was an effect that is not possible upon earth for the shafts of coloured light streamed from all three directions at once, forming a perfect blend in the middle of the apartment.

And so, to bring this account to an end, which I fancy has already been far too protracted, was our new room added to the house. An extremely small event in an extremely large world, but I give it that you may see how life deals with us here in these particular realms, and to provide you with some idea of what lies before you in pleasurable enjoyment and contentment of mind when it so happens that you, my friends, will come to join us in these lands.

What I have told you in the preceding account is but a commonplace incident in lives that are, however, anything but commonplace. For if these realms of which I speak were to appear commonplace to us, we should soon betake ourselves to other parts, or energetically earn the right to do so. Never for one moment, since I became an inhabitant of the spirit world, have I found the time to drag, as you would say; never have I been at a loose end for somewhat to do; never have I been bored with circumstances.

Life, indeed, is full to the brim with activities of many kinds. Truly can [say that I have never worked so hard in my life since I came to live in the spirit world! I always thought I could do a good day's work when I was on earth, and indeed, my friends there all declared that it was overwork that finally took me off the earth altogether.

The truth is that it is not only an increase in our labours here of which we are sensible, but the capacity and energy for 'increased output' to use your present idiom, that seem illimitable. And as the work remains to be done, well—we just do it!

Now, as I promised at the beginning, to the changes that have taken place in these realms themselves. Such changes that have occurred are not sensational for we have undergone no great upheavals such as you have on earth. You cannot pass through the 'trials and tribulations' of two great wars without many corresponding changes taking place. With us, of course, it is utterly different. Life here goes on placidly, without interruption or interference. Nothing can upset our economy, under which term I would designate the whole immense organisation of these realms, so that as we pass our lives here we see houses built, and houses being removed, not in large numbers, but here and there as the circumstances demand.

Were we a world that had only itself to consider, were we completely shut off from earth, the case would be different, perhaps. But my friends will remember that every soul that lives upon earth must eventually come for all time into spirit land! During normal times upon earth, the many organisations in the spirit world are fully capable of dealing with the usual influx of folk into these lands. But bethink you what happens when universal war breaks out on earth, and people pass to us not in hundreds of thousands but in *tens of millions*. The normal influx becomes a torrent.

There is no real need for us each, individually, to work harder for there are so many eager and willing to augment our usual numbers as to allow for all contingencies. But while we ourselves can be supplemented in our services without any strain being placed upon the community of these realms, the homes of rest, as they exist and function during normal terrestrial conditions, become totally inadequate. For you will know that most folk, as they come here at their dissolution, need rest in more or less degree according to the circumstances and manner of their passing.

The period of rest varies from what would be a few days to what would be a few months if we were to judge such things by earthly computations. For example, my own passing was not attended by any distressing conditions distressing, that is, to myself—and so my period of rest was exceedingly brief. But the thousands upon thousands whose dissolution is caused by war are an altogether different case. They have frequently undergone a severe shock. They have, in every sense of the term, been projected into the spirit world, and that is an irregularity for the spirit body itself. It was not meant to do that, but to pass naturally and gently into these lands.

The earth (officially) thinks and believes that once a person has 'died' then there is nothing more to be done. (I am not considering now, of course, such beliefs as 'prayers for the dead' and so on). Wars kill off people in their thousands, and they have passed out of sight of the full majority of incarnate man. Later on, I shall have a few more words to speak to you upon this important aspect of the subject. For the present, it devolves upon us in the spirit world to care for all these millions of souls—*tens of millions of souls*—who have come to us prematurely, before they have lived their normal span of years upon earth. Needless to remind you that the spirit world does not fail humanity.

When your wars commence upon earth, the word is given to us that new homes of rest must be built in readiness for the hideous slaughter that is to take place. Spaces are vast here so there is no lack of room in which to build the most beautiful homes of rest, where, in addition to those already existing, the tortured mind and the riven body may regain their calm, and become rested and re-invigorated. Such buildings as these, and the demand has been for many of them, are built rapidly, but they omit nothing.

When the use for them dwindles and finally ceases, they are removed, but temporary though they may be, nothing is forgotten or omitted that will make the buildings themselves beautiful and their efficiency of the highest. Transient as they are, they must not be roughly put up; they must accord in every detail with the permanent beauties of these realms.

That is the great change that takes place among us, my friends. Sensational—no. Vital and urgent—yes. Would that it were never necessary. For here are we rectifying the colossal blunders of the earth people. But just so long as man in his abysmal folly tolerates wars, then just so long will it be necessary for us to erect these great new homes of rest for the dwellers of earth who have been driven forth from their earthly lives into the spirit world through the wicked acts of man.

Recently, we have seen the removal of numbers of these rest homes. We are not sorry to see them go for with their departure it means that the need for them has departed too, and that gives us good cause for great joy.

When I tell you that otherwise there are no changes for me to note, you must not infer that we have got into a groove, so to speak, that we are 'behind the times' or that we are perfectly content 'to go on in the same old way' and that therefore our lives must be one unending, dreary, monotony. That is most certainly not the case.

We are intensely alive, joyfully happy, always occupied upon something useful to our neighbours, and as for being behind the times, why, it is you who are that for we are ahead of them, always ahead of them as you will experience for yourself one of these days. Then you will see that I have not overstated the case, but most decidedly *understated* it!

Past, Present, Future

A subject that exercises many wise minds is that of 'the past, the present, and the future', as regarded from the earthly point of view. It is sometimes asked at what precise moment does the present become the past, and similarly, when does the future become the present?

Some will liken a person's life upon earth to a pencil drawn across a sheet of paper, the black line left by the pencil being the past, the point of the pencil in contact with the paper, the immediate present while the blank page before it is the future. What I think is of most importance to us now is the view held by many that the spirit world, having no cognisance of time, measured or otherwise (as it is supposed), the present and the past are one.

One cannot but feel sympathy with this conception when one recalls the generally accepted idea of 'heaven' where 'the company of the blessed', the angels and saints, are doomed—and I am persuaded that is the right word to use—to spend the whole of eternity singing hymns and other spiritual songs. In such case the past would be indistinguishable from the present, one would imagine, while the future—a bleak outlook— would promise not the slightest difference from either the present or the past. However, we have something more substantial upon which to deliberate, and that is our memory, a function of the mind which would be of precious little value in an eternity of such vocalistic efforts as I have just noted.

Those of us in the spirit world who have lived upon earth have a full and complete memory of all that transpired with us when we were incarnate. That memory is perfect. All the events and experiences of our lives, our thoughts and deeds, are infallibly and indelibly impressed upon the tablets of the mind. But that is not to say that in our lives here we are constantly in the presence, as it were, of our whole earthly lives, that we are haunted by the whole immense contents of our memories. Life under such conditions would become a veritable nightmare, and our heavens would instantly be transformed into hells. Our minds would be a complete phantasmagoria of thoughts and ideas, with the remembrance of an uncountable series of events of the most heterogeneous order, the trivial being intermixed with the important.

No, my friends; things are much better ordered than that. Our memories are tenacious and exact, but we are not everlastingly beset by the whole contents of our minds. We can delve into the past as we wish. If we have done those things on earth which we have later come to regret when we are permanent residents of these lands and so retarded our progress, then we shall have no reluctance to recall them that, by our present deeds, we may offset those unhappy incidents.

But, it may be asked, if we have no time in the spirit world how can there be a past as it is understood on earth? It is true we have no night, but eternal day; no winter, but perpetual summer. We have no measurement of time by means of clocks and calendars. Life is therefore a continuous, literally continuous, succession of existence, and that you might feel inclined to say, is all that there is to be said about it. No past, no future, but one eternal ever present now. Let us see if the 'no past' is really a true statement, though I must remind you that we have a cognisance of the passage of time.

When I first spoke to you, it was some years ago. You know that. And so do I. To me in these realms it is in the past, and to me it was—and still is—a most memorable event. It enabled me to set right something that I ought never to have done when I was incarnate. Am I not forever grateful for the opportunity of so doing? Indeed, I am. Nor am I, as far as I can foretell, ever likely to forget that past event.

How does it present itself to me, this memory of the past? Why, in exactly the same way as does your memory present its past to you. As far as my memory is concerned I can say—and this is essentially a personal experience—I can say that I detect no difference whatever between my memory functions when I was incarnate and my memory functions now that I have resided in the spirit world all these years of your measured time. (With the actual contents of the memory we are not precisely concerned at the moment).

Since I have been in these lands a multiplicity of events have happened to me, as to all the other folk here. They have happened, they are past, though all the particulars of them are readily capable of being recalled to the mind—recollected—upon the instant. Most emphatically they are not of the present with me any more than the actions which you performed or the experiences which you underwent yesterday are present with you today other than as a memory. The effect of those actions and experiences may, of course, abide with you for a long time, but that is another matter altogether.

As I look back over the past since my advent here, I can recall all manner of the most pleasant things, occurrences, experiences, and so on. So clearly can I recall them that a few years ago we recorded some of them, even as we are now recording this for you. In writing them down, I used the past tense, not only because from your point of view they were in the past, but because from my point of view also were they in the past.

Death?—the spirit teachers say, there is no death. What seems so is but a transition to another world and life is continuous, without break. Death is a mere discarding of the physical body. That is a spiritual truth. A continuity of life, and most decidedly a continuity of memory. Where there is memory, there is past. Of what use memory if there were no past to remember?

History is comprised of events and the people concerned in or with them. Events of a national character will be set down in the earth's chronicles. The events themselves are past, though their repercussions may extend a long way in time until you feel or observe them in these present days. By reading of these events you can bring them before the mind's-eye, and the descriptive powers of the writer may be able to afford you some insight into the principal characters involved in them. That a great deal of inaccuracy has become interwoven with the historical narratives is only to be expected. The absolute truths of history are only to be found within the libraries of the spirit world.

In the city, which I can see from my windows here, I have in leisure moments browsed among volumes of history. My interest is not entirely idle because when I was a writer on earth I sometimes used the events of history as the main theme for a book. The history I introduced was as accurate as it was possible to have it, and according to the standard works upon the subject. For the rest I drew upon my imagination in the purely fictional parts of my work, with the historical minutiae to give some substance of verisimilitude.

Sometimes when I have dipped into the history books in the city library I have been amazed to read for the first time the true account of particular events, some of them actually narrated by the leading participants. This, however, is by the way.

All you have upon earth are the chronicles of the world's events. But here in the spirit world are existing all the persons, great and small, famous and infamous, good and bad, male and female, who are but names, and names only, to you still incarnate. They are widely dispersed throughout this world: some in the heights, others are still languishing deep in the depths, and who, from my own observations, seem likely to remain there for heaven alone knows how much longer.

All your ancestors, my friends, are here somewhere. It is nothing, therefore, during the course of one's days here—I use that phrase metaphorically, you will understand—literally to encounter someone who dwelt upon earth many, many years agone, in times which are now regarded as historical by the incarnate. I have had a number of very pleasant experiences in this way. My musical interests have led me into most delightful company among master musicians, some of whom flourished in early times and others of more recent days. The musicians, like other crafts in these lands, have formed a society of themselves, a very ancient one, to which new members are added from time to time, although the entrance of master musicians from the earth world has perceptibly dwindled!

With a number of the master musicians I have been closely associated—a case of wheels within wheels. Many have been the delectable forgatherings which we have had at my house. Here were to be seen—and spoken with—musicians of different ages of the earth's history. A sort of fusion of the past with the present.

There was no mistake about the past, though. These good men have all of them somewhat to relate of their earthly lives.

One of the most interesting links with the past—interesting, at least, to me—is connected with my house. You must know that its counterpart on earth is an ancient domicile, retreating into the historical times of the land. Imagine my surprise when a most genial man presented himself to me as a former owner of the very house in which I lived on earth, when the building itself was young in years. He had seen my present house here in course of erection, and though the materials of which it is constructed differ widely from earthly materials, yet there was something about it that seemed familiar to him.

An exchange of information proved him right, and nothing would satisfy him but that I should show him over the whole house. I was happy to do so, in exchange for which he gave me some personal details about himself, and made some observations upon the times in which he lived. Now it may be asked, if the earthly counterpart of my house is historically old, why has it been left to me to possess a similar house in the spirit world? What of the desires of the tenants or owners previous to my tenure of it? Privilege of some sort? Indeed, no.

The answer is simply that the preceding tenants or owners of the earthly house had no wish for a spirit-world counterpart when they came here to live. Assuming the right to possess, there was nothing whatever to debar them, even if all of them had been of like mind, and all had decided to erect similar houses for themselves. It means that there would have been a number of houses of identical pattern instead of just the one in which I am dwelling. Their particular taste in a home for themselves had altered. It had merely transpired that way.

The interest which the former owner has expressed in my house is therefore purely a passing one. He has admired it, of course, for the vivid contrast it presents to its earthly shadow. To refer to a solid house of bricks and plaster as a shadow may raise a smile upon your face, but I assure you that to me now, my present house is far more substantial than ever my earthly one was when I was actually living in it!

How often are the questions asked upon earth: do ghosts exist, and have you ever seen one? We can answer that for you. Yes, ghosts do exist, and you are they! We have seen you. However, we seem to be getting off our true course, and I must restrain my fatal habit of digressing!

This previous owner of my earthly house often calls to see us, and we have fallen to discussing the times in which he lived. There is something extremely pleasant in chatting with a man who lived in a bygone age, when life was simpler, but in many respects more hazardous. My friend had found that the safest way of securing his tenure of earthly life to its fullest extent was studiously to refrain from airing his opinions except upon matters that were manifestly innocuous, such as music and the arts or agriculture and kindred subjects, and to leave religion and politics resolutely alone.

He found it healthier for his mind's sake to leave the cities and towns unvisited, or to make such visits as were unavoidable as brief as possible, and to remain in the country places and attend to his own affairs. Thus he was able to preserve not only his peace of mind, but his earthly life as well. How much blood was unnecessarily shed in the cause of politics and religion, the history books amply reveal. As each party came into power, it was responsible for the production of 'martyrs to the faith' upon the opposite side. Had the truth been known in those days the martyrs of religion would have also known that they were sacrificing their earthly lives in a mistaken cause, and so saved themselves.

But surely, it will be queried, a man who gives up his earthly life for his faith, whatever that faith may be and however mistaken, cannot have thrown his life away? He must have reaped some benefit of spiritual value. Now who would you think to be the best judge of that? Wishing for an answer to this question, my friend and I sought and interrogated one who is still revered upon earth as a martyr and has since been elevated to sainthood—preferment which he refuses to accept!

In the light of spiritual verity, he says, he was wholly mistaken. By refusing to subscribe to certain enactments, both religious and political, which by tyrannous means were being forced upon the people, he forfeited his earthly life. It was, in fact, an encroachment of the law into matters where it had no right to be, and the law in those days, in such cases, meant the head of the state. It was not that he was fighting for freedom in a general sense but for another religious system, which he believed to be the only and true one, but which, after his entry into spirit lands, he discovered was not true by any means. He had, indeed, supported a false cause. He thought he was grasping the substance only to find that it was a shadow. The articles to which he was ordered to subscribe his name were the outcome of political expediency, and the very religion which they opposed were false.

The role of 'martyr for the faith' is a profitless and thankless one as seen by the light of spirit truths and spirit laws. Whatever may be the opinions of my earthly friends upon such things, there are always the pronounced views of the person chiefly concerned—the martyr himself—to be considered. If he expresses the view that he made a useless and needless sacrifice, who shall gainsay him in the light of spiritual verity? If our eyes are firmly shut, we may blunder badly, or imagine ourselves to be in deadly peril where we tread, only to find upon opening our eyes that we are, figuratively speaking, in open country far from any obstacle likely to cause us accident.

But surely, it may still be countered, there would be some compensation for the suffering which that person endured? Of course. But that is another matter entirely. Homes of rest have not sprung up in these lands during the last few years only. They have existed time out of mind, and many a martyr of ages past has found himself safely within the shelter of one of them after his turbulent passing. His intentions were of the best, but his views were mistaken, and in sacrificing himself for an empty cause he gained no spiritual reward in the shape of a 'heavenly crown', such as the devout like to believe is the case, but insofar as he lived a good life in the service of others, his violent and premature advent into spirit lands would receive ample compensation, while he would reap the good harvest which he sowed upon earth.

One must always remember too, as my friendly informant of other days pointed out to me, that, generally speaking, feelings ran higher in those days. There was a certain measure of stubbornness not to be perceived in these later times while fanaticism was taken at its word, so to speak, and given the chance to prove itself. It did so in the form of martyrdom. The minds of people were in many respects only partly formed; they were superstitious to a degree, and utterly incapable of distinguishing a very ordinary natural happening from some alleged supernatural manifestation.

On so many occasions such folk precipitated themselves into inextricable difficulties by what would be regarded 1n these wiser times as 'sheer stupidity'. As for those who were in direct communication with us here, their position was parlous indeed, for any thought of intercourse with the 'dead' was simply an abomination since it was taught and believed that the good people in 'heaven' would not dream of such wicked practices as being against Holy Writ—a notion which has its partisans to this day—so that it was only left to the devils out of hell, which one must avoid like the plague.

Some indeed had the courage to speak the truth, but the flames of the stake soon stifled their blasphemous and heretical utterances. You have much to be thankful for, my good friends, in these present times, the dreadful pains you have undergone notwithstanding. However, let us not dwell over long in the past, but turn to the future.

Mercifully, you would perhaps say, the future is a closed book. If the whole were to be thrown open for all to see, many would predict that chaos would prevail. Yet one hears of numerous cases where the future has been accurately predicted. How does that come about?

First, I would like to observe how strange it is that such great importance should be attached to any predictive utterances that may emanate from the spirit world. It so often happens that more weight is attached to this particular type of communication than many another, if the prediction should be completely fulfilled. It would appear to establish the speaker's bona fides in a remarkable way. Any spirit person, in effect, who correctly predicts a certain event, whether of personal or public application, seems at once to have proved himself reliable, accurate, and altogether a desirable person.

The opposite, of course, is an abomination; a deceiver, an impersonator of good, but an imposter, or what is worst of all, a devil. That would make the good people from the spirit world infallible, a distinction which we beg leave to disclaim utterly. Conversely, if we err in some statement, then we are evil, which is equally untrue.

If we have no measurement of time in the spirit world, how can we speak of the future and give any substance to our words? Yet we have a future before us, as you will have gathered from what I have said to you in these and other writings, for how can spiritual progression have any meaning whatsoever if there be no future in which to gain it? Those unhappy souls in the lowest realms of darkness whose numbers have been so increased of late years—all those creatures of misery have a future before them.

Time for them has stood still, seemingly, since the moment of their entry into those noisome regions. Time is of no account to them whatever. Some of them have been in that state for hundreds of years. But every soul there, no matter how debased he may be, no matter how low he has sunk, can lift himself out of his misery, and will ultimately do so, though it may take aeons of time in the process. But the future lies before each single soul in darkness, as it does before us all, and in that future lies also the potentiality of rising to the greatest heights. What are the limits to spiritual progression? There is none here who would dare to hazard a guess.

The conception that we live in an eternal present is a wrong one. We all of us hope for the future. Observe how many of us there are who have our hopes fulfilled to the last detail. The number is uncountable. The greater our endeavours, the more we achieve, and so much the quicker will be our progression. Circumstances over which we have no control, to use a common phrase, may retard the fulfilment of our wishes, but there is much with which one can occupy one's self in the meantime. My own case will afford an example for you.

When I first came to these lands and discovered the truth, I was troubled in mind by one book which I had written on earth, and which, unfortunately for me, could not now be unwritten. What was to be done? The thought came to me that if I might return to earth and speak the truth as I now knew it to be, I could counteract the unfairness and inaccuracies which I had set down, for the book dealt with this very subject of communicating with the spirit world.

Help and advice were soon forthcoming, and from a source that, in my most sanguine moments, I could never have dreamed possible. But such is the way of the spirit world that help, earnestly sought, can and does come from the very highest sources. My request was granted, but there was one qualification. If I wished to communicate with the earth, I should have to wait for such time in the future when circumstances would allow of it. Various minor events would first have to take place in the lives of several people. In the intervening period, I could occupy myself variously to my own benefit. Here was a case where I had one eye, as you say, upon the future in a very specific way.

At last came the day whereon I was able to break my silence. What was once a future event became very much a present event, and now it has receded into the past, where I regard it just as do you any event in your life. You have your 'red-letter days', and so do we. This was one of mine.

What of the interim period of waiting for my wish to

be fulfilled, you may ask ? My wise friends and advisers placed me in full possession of all the facts and circumstances. Although I never actually communicated with the earth before the moment of my 'new' writing, yet I was conversant with all that was taking place among the different folk who would be, as it were, drawn into the accomplishment of my great desire. I was, therefore, aware of the passage of time on earth, and that events were steadily leading up to a focal point where I should be told: now you may speak.

That will lead to a further question: how was it known that my wish would be fulfilled? You would say that it was a prophecy without a doubt. But whence did it come, and from whom? Now that, in good truth, is something that I have always wondered myself, and I am no nearer finding a conclusive answer. All that one can say at this juncture is that in the upper realms of the spirit world there live beings who are infinitely wiser than we are, and that their knowledge is correspondingly great. Their knowledge and wisdom combined will enable them to make an accurate prognosis based upon an accurate diagnosis. But this must not be regarded in any way as fatalism or predestination.

As I view things now from my accumulated experience, I can see that there were many incidental happenings, contingencies, cross currents, as it were, that could have completely upset the plans and arrangements which were to culminate in my writing again. The ever-present and ever-to-be-respected free will of others was chief among them. But it so happened that at no time, nor upon any occasion, did the arrangements conflict with the wishes or sentiments of anyone, therefore that part of the scheme was concluded without hitch or setback.

It was known, without the slightest doubt, that we should meet with no serious obstruction or other impediment upon the way which could not be successfully overcome. As soon as the chain of events began drawing to a close, I had a still clearer perception of all that was afoot that would lead to ultimate success. I called to mind the old terms of official sanction: *nihil obstat: imprimatur.*

There was, however, one slight demur that we encountered, and that came from my earthly amanuensis. It was, in his opinion, a most unpropitious time in which to contemplate such a design. War had been let loose upon the world, people's minds were inevitably diverted to matters of a thoroughly material nature, and altogether (in his opinion, but not in ours!) the outlook was gloomy and the chances of success problematical. We were soon able to dispose of that, however, because we were sure of our ground.

Well, now, I have presented these details to you—I hope without tedium—to show that such prevision of the future as we are able to give on occasion, at least in such material matters as we have here discussed, is based upon a number of definite factors, and not upon some mysterious and very elusive condition of affairs, or upon the operation of a strange, complex, and incomprehensible law, whereby future events are set down in some book of chronological records, each awaiting inevitable fulfilment.

Nor can we, in some abstruse way, project our minds into the infinity of time, choose some event from the collection of shadows of future occurrences, and then tell you all about it. Vague, incomplete, and unsatisfactory as this description is, yet it is by some folk deemed to be something of an attempted explanation of any foreknowledge of future happenings.

What the whole truth is, I do not know, but I can tell you this. After leaving the earth world, we do not instantly become endowed with profound knowledge, but we are able to exercise the powers of our minds, and we can sometimes see into the minds of earth people.

Upon the knowledge we have thus gleaned, we are able to declare that certain results will be observable upon a given situation, but without detailing the chain of events and circumstances which will eventually lead to those results. We could find an analogy, though an elementary one, in a particular service widely known upon earth—and equally widely abused—namely, your weather forecasts. If you have a number of observers situated in different parts of the country, and who, at given times, are prepared to send reports of the weather conditions in their particular district and its surroundings to a central office, a sound idea of the prevailing weather of the whole country can be gained. Experts can then give a fairly correct forecast of future conditions.

But if only one announcement were made during the period of twenty-four hours, much might have happened in the meantime of which you would be completely unaware, and which would falsify the whole forecast. For a certain tendency had been noted by the observers which, had it persisted, would have upheld the original forecast, but some new condition had set in—the wind, for example, blew from another direction—and so altered the entire meteorological prognosis.

When you consider the mutability of men's minds, is it to be wondered at that certain trends, which we perceive in some person's affairs, may be so influenced as to upset any mildly predictive statement that we may make? The truth is that few people on earth are fully aware of the extent to which their material concerns are assisted and advanced by their unseen friends of the spirit world. We do our best to give what aid we can, without. at the same time, taking complete charge of your earthly lives, which would be wrong and is utterly forbidden.

Furthering your affairs involves much work upon our part, where we must gently influence minds in your favour. As we see things progressing, we are able to give you some account of our efforts and their probable outcome. We say, in effect, that as things stand at this moment, all is moving favourably, and we have every hope of accomplishing our aims, whatever they may be, for your benefit. Then, before we have the opportunity to speak with you again, some incident, small in itself, but large in its consequences, may obtrude and wholly belie our previous words.

Naturally, you are disappointed, and perhaps a little distrustful of our utterances, though not necessarily of our intentions. It is obvious, you might say to yourself, that our unseen friends cannot do all they feel or wish they could do. Our prestige is apt to drop somewhat!— while the fault rests, in good truth, not with us, but with the changeable and sometimes uncertain mind of man.

Perhaps it would be a wise precaution, when we come to discuss our earthly friends' affairs with them, if we added some proviso or another to protect ourselves in case of complete or partial failure.

I am reminded of the time when I was incarnate. As a popular preacher I covered a deal of ground, both literally and theologically, though of the latter the least said the better! In consequence, railway time-tables were familiar to me. Now what would you think if upon every time-table you perceived some such notice as this,

'While every effort is made to see that all trains depart strictly on time, we cannot guarantee that any train will arrive on time or, indeed, that it will arrive at all'?

During the extremes of winter weather, the prompt arrival of trains may be a hazardous affair. That is something of which I need scarcely remind you. There is always that unhappy eventuality, an accident, which may prevent your arrival at your destination. Yet time-tables in their way are a series of printed prophecies upon which one has come to place a degree of reliance, without pausing to consider that a very small incident can falsify any of its statements. Men's minds can, indeed, bring the whole railway system to a stoppage, a situation not unheard of, you will agree.

So you see that the outcome of any plans or arrangements into which you may enter with our help are beset with complications of one sort or another, any one of which might overthrow the whole, and compel a fresh start, perhaps from the very beginning. In giving you what we believe to be an ultimate result, we do so without admitting you to a knowledge of the train of events leading up to the conclusion. That is as well since from over-eagerness you might be tempted into precipitate action of your own and completely spoil matters.

I am persuaded that beings in the highest realms are fully acquainted with all that lies before the individual as well as before the world in general. Perhaps you may think that spirit people might have something better to do than interest themselves so closely with terrestrial affairs. We have plenty to do, certainly, but what we do for the earth and its people is done in service and not because we lack employment, or because we are interfering busybodies. It is done because the earth world plays an important part in the universal scheme of life, and because, without the help of the spirit world, the earth would find itself in deep distress.

Though the beings of those exalted realms know what lies in the future, that is not to say that the whole future is pre-ordained, fixed, and immutable, and, as it were, irrevocably inscribed upon some gigantic cosmic chart or map. I believe the truth rests in the vast knowledge of every kind that these great personages possess, and that such knowledge can be passed down through a complete and unbroken chain of people until it reaches us in these lower realms. That is my opinion, and as such I give it to you.

I am not just drawing upon my imagination for this, but basing it upon my own experiences of these wise souls, whose knowledge is simply prodigious, unbelievable. I have had demonstrations of it in affairs of my own, which I thought too insignificant to be worthy of their least attention. But I was completely wrong in thinking thus.

When I first broached the question of communicating with the earth, the subject was referred to a 'higher authority'. Since then, I have visited this very personage, in company with Edwin and Ruth, in his home in the highest realms. It is no exaggeration to say that we were amazed at the immense grasp he had of our simple affairs. We could not believe for one moment that he had merely been 'primed', as you would say, with full information concerning our three selves. While we know he is not possessed of all knowledge, yet we have ample evidence that his knowledge is enormous.

Again it may be asked, why should an illustrious being, such as I describe him to be, show such knowledge of three people who are situated spiritually leagues from him? All I can say is that if we were the only three people so circumstanced then it would be both remarkable and inexplicable, but most emphatically we are not. His knowledge is used for the benefit of the whole of these realms—and far beyond. And there is his wisdom as well. It is the application of both, that we all of us experience here.

I have chatted upon this subject with many friends, and we are all convinced that from the great reservoir of knowledge and wisdom in these high realms there comes the inspiration that is diffused throughout the spirit world, which in turn is transmitted to the earth world. For the scientist here will tell you that when he asks for guidance in his labours, that guidance comes in tangible form from some other realm. He knows not the direction whence it comes; all he knows is that come it does—without failure. The same thing applies to the engineer, or the musician; the painter, or the architect, and to all the numerous other departments of human endeavour.

We may seem to have wandered far from our theme, the future, but in reality we have not, for I have been trying to probe things a little for you, to seek to discover whence or how any foreknowledge of the future can be derived. This we can be sure of, namely, that being endowed with free will, each one of us, without exception, our various and respective paths are not laid down for us as though we were some locomotive engine confined to a permanent way from which we cannot deviate.

That we have an ultimate destiny, there is no possible doubt, namely, that we should so progress spiritually that at last we shall attain to the highest heaven and so to the greatest happiness. But we shall each of us reach that great altitude by a myriad different ways.

Our course is more easily perceived when we become

residents of the spirit world. While we are incarnate our vision is limited—very limited—but we can always claim the right to exercise our free will, and none has the right to prevent us. It is true that with an individual's co-operation we may suggest and map out a certain road for him, whereon to travel his earthly journey, and we may do all we can to further that aim, but should the object of our interest or endeavours express his disapproval and wish to go upon his own way, it is forbidden that we should do otherwise than allow him to make his choice and exercise his free will.

You must know that after we have passed from earth into these beautiful realms of the spirit world, we have undergone an experience which yet awaits you, and we are that much the better informed. We have advanced a little further along the road than have you, and we are upon rising ground where our vision is less restricted and our outlook is wider, more comprehensive, and where we can draw in full measure upon the many wise minds who dwell here.

It is completely wrong to attach so much importance to predictive utterances, as though the whole subject and practice of communication between the spirit world and the earth world depended upon them. There are many empty minds upon earth who fondly believe that if they were given a correct forecast of the result of some sporting event, they have thereby proved that there is such a place as a spirit world, and that there are such things—as they call us!—as spirit people. They fancy they have achieved something, when in reality they have proved nothing beyond their own stupidity, which was never in question.

What of their departed relatives and friends? Are they to be regarded as living only among the great ones of the highest heaven? Perhaps in their presumption they imagine so. Would they deem the accurate forecast of sporting results as sufficient to establish the identity and bona fides of their cherished friends who have passed on before them? Dear me, no. That would never do; that sort of thing is preposterous. Their relatives would not communicate. All of which is remarkably silly, my dear friends.

We are not here in the spirit world especially to think for you nor to place certain people with trivial minds in possession of information which would give them a material advantage over their neighbours. It is only necessary to answer such fools according to their folly. We are not 'soothsayers', but we are anxious to help our friends on earth to surmount the many difficulties incidental to their earthly lives, to smooth the way a little.

And that is all part of the grand scheme for our spiritual progression.

Colour

About half-way along a passage upon the upper floor of our house there is a small bay in which a brief flight of stairs leads to a door. Through this door I have taken many friends, especially new arrivals in spirit lands, for this door opens directly upon a section of flat roof.

From here a magnificent view is to be gained of a great tract of the countryside, with the city gleaming in the distance. To those who have not as yet travelled through these realms, or at least this small segment of them, the view from the roof comes as something of an inspiring revelation to them. With scarcely an exception, we receive the same reply to a question which one or other of us delights in putting to our new visitor, namely: what strikes you most forcibly as you gaze upon this scene? The answer: the riot of colour.

Most assuredly, that is so. It is a sight which never fails to fill us with fresh wonder and charm, seasoned residents though we be. The reason is to be found not only in the delight to the physical sense of sight, but what is more important in many ways, the colour itself is exhilarating. This feeling of exhilaration is not some doubtful spiritual experience, intangible and apt to evaporate after a brief while. It is much more than that. It rejuvenates one, even in these realms of juvenility. It braces one up, as you would say, and acts like a tonic.

The contrast between our world and yours in this matter of colour alone is tremendous. The two worlds are not to be compared. Indeed, what the earth lacks and needs most urgently in some quarters, is colour, a vast deal more colour. Your towns are drab, dreary, and toneless. Perhaps I shall be taken to task for that statement, but you must remember that I once lived upon earth, and that I am now living in the spirit world.

My statement is a comparative one. Were you to have even the most fleeting glimpse of these realms, you would at once be convinced. Bethink you of the dingy state of your buildings. You will, of course, appreciate that I am speaking of normal times on earth and not of now, after all the horrors of war have left their grim marks, and the years of enforced neglect have added to the murkiness.

When your buildings are first erected, they stand in their pristine freshness, and they are more or less tolerable because they are clean, and free from the grime which is bound in time to envelop them. Some folk will admire the dark greyness of the ancient buildings, such as the great Gothic cathedrals. They will say that time has mellowed the newness of the stone, and added beauty and grandeur to the masterpieces of olden days.

As an expressed opinion, one is bound to respect it, but I can say this: wait until you see one of our buildings, and the force of my remarks will make itself manifest. You would instantly exclaim how glad you are to know that no grime and dirt can come, no structural dilapidations, to spoil the eternal beauty of our masterpieces of architecture, or of even the simplest and most unpretentious cottage .

It is true, of course, that you have such a condition of affairs on earth as we could not have here. The smoke of the towns and cities, for example, which quickly makes the buildings dull and dirty. But the time will come when smoke will no longer be present to constitute the menace it is at present. Other methods will be devised, and the smoke will vanish never to reappear. At least that would ensure that your towns are clean as far as its buildings are concerned. But the colour will still be missing if nothing is done about it.

The tendency through the passage of years on earth has been towards less and less colour, and nowhere is this more noticeable than in the very clothes you wear. There was a time on earth when folk wore the gayest and brightest colours. This was not left to the women-folk alone for the men were equally gayly habited.

If people on earth knew the real value and influence of colour upon the mind, and thence upon the body, which would in turn react upon a whole nation, they would be literally astonished. You will understand that I am not advocating some new essay in dress reform, though there is ample room for that too!

The men are the worst offenders for their clothes are drab and uninspiring from the colour point of view. I am persuaded that the most dismal and lugubrious experience is to stand before an audience or congregation of clergymen, all attired in their clerical black—that is how it seems to me now. Nothing could be more funereal and suggestive of everything that is melancholy and depressing. Certainly some of the clergy have become a little bolder since my days on earth, and with great daring have clothed themselves in sober—very sober—grey. At least that is a turn in the right direction, but religion should be happy and cheerful, and the ministers of it should be attired so as to proclaim that fact. So much that is associated with religion is clothed in black.

Never was the deterioration in the use of colour on earth more noticeable than in the spirit world. For when people arrive here and wear the clothes to which they were accustomed when incarnate, they look utterly incongruous because their clothes are colourless. Usually it is not long before they change to their new mode of dress.

That is a matter we do not press upon our newly arrived friends, but the instant they *feel* out of place in their old earthly habiliments, the change takes place. There are exceptions, though very few, I recall when my former ecclesiastical superior, a 'prince of the Church', came to reside here. Following the usual custom, he wore his earthly clothes, by which you will understand that I mean their counterpart. As they were already rich and colourful they looked splendid in these surroundings, so much so that he was persuaded not to discard them just yet. And, of course, he felt perfectly comfortable so attired. Wherever he went, people who did not know him personally or by repute, knew him for what he had been on earth. Eventually, however, he donned his spirit attire which was equally colourful and gracious to the eye.

In the spirit world, colour plays a vital part in our lives for it provides us not only with visual enjoyment, but from colour come musical sounds of surpassing beauty and purity. It also contributes towards the life-giving force from which we derive our very existence.

After spending so many years on earth attired in black, our clergymen friends of these and other realms are delighted when they can at last put it off for the natural brightness of their own spirit clothes.

So many of the religious denominations on earth have shunned any approach to colour, beyond stained glass windows, by abolishing the use of vestments which were at least pleasant to the eye. One Church, however, has retained them fully. Though their liturgical colours may be emblematical yet they serve a useful purpose by adding brightness and colour to the proceedings, whatever the true value of the latter may be.

Black makes its persistent appearance in the services for the 'dead', to give solemnity to observances which cannot be otherwise than awe-inspiring, for what could be more *awful* than *death*?—so it is thought. One *could* think of something far worse than death itself, and that is the special kind of heaven conjured up in the minds of some folk that is supposed to follow that death!

Black has come to be associated with the various trappings of dissolution, although once upon a time on earth the colour for mourning was not black but yellow. It is remarkable that some people once favoured this particular colour, for yellow is most decidedly a *soothing* colour for the incarnate if properly used, so that in days past when people like their brethren today were in sore distress at the loss of a dear one—for human affections have always persisted—the use of yellow attire will have exerted a calming and comforting influence upon them. There is everything to commend the use of this bright, cheerful colour in such circumstances. It would be far better had it never been displaced by black.

Colour upon earth presents a wide field for investigation for its potentialities are scarcely known. It can be made to exert a most beneficial influence upon the health and temperament of the incarnate if it is rightly employed.

Here in the spirit world colour is utilised particularly to bring back stability into troubled minds and in the treatment of folk whose passage into these lands has been violent or otherwise distressing. When I saw a rest home for the first time, I observed a shaft of blue light was descending upon and enveloping the whole edifice. This, I was told, would provide all that was necessary for initial treatment.

There are rays of many colours to be seen descending upon the homes of rest, each for its special purpose. It is not only the colour which produces the required results, but the elements of the ray itself. Indeed, the colour here plays a relatively minor part, though when the ray is actually perceived, the pleasant nature of the colour will bring a large measure of joy to the beholder.

When you come to consider the wide diversity of transitions and their causes, each calling for special treatment and care in the rest homes and elsewhere, you will see the need for the range of colours in the rays to be equally diverse. But as there is no end—or seemingly there is none—to the number of tints and blends which can be derived, you will see that ample provision is made for *every* type of transition.

These rays are wonderful to view in operation for the colours and their myriad blends are truly thrilling— there is no other word to describe them. You must understand they are *not* mere coloured light. The shades of blue, for instance. I have see them from the very darkest and richest to the palest and most delicate, and of such a nature that even the former was brilliant and bright, though darker than the deepest sapphire. You could not simulate this one colour on earth without reducing very greatly the illuminating power and extent of the light.

In the same way, you could not evolve the pale blue without losing brilliance and intensity of the colour. Excepting the light of the sun, of course, your light is otherwise artificial while ours is real and instinct with life. One could say that your light is dead, or rather, lifeless, while ours is living light. That applies to all colour in the spirit world, whether it be of the flowers, of the buildings, of the water, or of the clothes we wear. Colour with us means light; absence of colour means darkness.

A great many people on earth have what they call their favourite colour. So do we in the spirit world, even among the galaxy to be encountered upon every hand. Some will account for this particular partiality—I am speaking of you now—by averring that the colours themselves call to mind various pleasant circumstances. Folk will say, for instance, that yellow and its different tones pleases them most because yellow is a sunny colour and so reminds them of the summertime; others will prefer green, saying that it conjures up the meadows and fields and shady woods. Bright blue will put other folk in remembrance of the sea and clear skies while red makes some feel warm and comfortable, and so on. These diversified mental images could be multiplied almost without number. There is also another side to the story for some people will express great distaste for certain colours because they remind them of unpleasant things. With the latter we are not now concerned.

Such 'association of ideas' with colours provides one with a certain basis for the predilection, but the real reason lies much deeper than that. Just as your physical body will give all outward signs that it requires some special but easily acquired element to keep it in good health, so does the *higher* self require that which is part of its very substance—namely, colour. This need becomes translated into a predilection for the colour it needs. In speaking of the higher self, I would ask you to remember that every single soul, incarnate and discarnate alike, has the divine element within him.

It may be so crushed by a gross nature and gross living as to be almost extinct, but absolutely extinct it can never be. Even in those awful dark regions where everything is of the foulest, there yet resides within every one of those unhappy souls that celestial element—call it the divine spark, if you wish. That can never, in any circumstances, die or be extinguished. It is from that microscopic gleam that progress will commence, though it may take thousands of years of earthly time before it shows the least sign of activity, of increasing.

The higher self will be manifest in a variety of ways, including that special taste for a certain colour. With you on earth it means that some one colour or another is required in your etheric counterpart, which is thus reached through the physical body, and it reveals itself in this way by implanting in you a preference for a specific colour. The colour which you so favour is completely in *tune* with you, hence the unmistakable feeling of warmth towards that colour.

If it should, in the process, call to mind such agreeable things as the sea, or the woods, or sunny days, and so on, then so much the better for such imaginings will help to strengthen your preference for that colour and so lead you to introduce and employ it, or its different shades, whenever it is practicable. By doing so, you will derive excellent benefit both physically and mentally. What is yet more important, your etheric body, for which your physical body is but the visible covering, will also benefit.

You will perhaps say that, as things are at present conducted, it is not always easy to incorporate one's favourite colour in such measure as is necessary. Men, indeed, with their excessively colourless and drab clothing, and with their customary diffidence of anything that is not strictly in accordance with prescribed ideas, will feel that the colour question is an impossible one for them, beyond introducing some little extra colour into their homes.

That is a situation which, there is every hope, will be fully remedied in the future. It undoubtedly will take some time because of that diffidence to which I have just alluded. But the change to more colourful apparel will become a universal movement in due course. I am not pretending to prophesy, but solely giving you *some* idea of a general trend which will be noticed, we are persuaded, before too long.

From this trend it is possible to perceive—according as I have discussed with you a little earlier in these present writings—what we all hope in the spirit world will eventually come to pass, and that is the better and more adequate introduction of colour into your whole life upon earth. It matters not whether it be in your clothing or your buildings so long as the colour is there.

When smoke has been so abated as to vanish altogether from your cities and towns, your buildings will have a better chance of preserving some of their initial cleanliness of surface. You will still have the fumes from vehicular traffic to pollute the air, but that minor problem will also be solved in its proper season. Nothing then stands in the path of making your cities truly beautiful by the wholesale introduction of colour, properly applied and properly blended, into all your edifices.

You cannot imagine, you will say, what on earth a beautiful Gothic cathedral would look like if it were in colour. Hideous, and possibly vulgar; monstrous, you might be tempted to declare. Think of a pink cathedral, or a purple one. Why, the whole idea is ludicrous. Is it really so? Not by any manner of means, my dear friends.

The trouble is that such introduction of colour would be so very unusual to you because you have grown accustomed to being more or less without it. Now you may say that there are certain parts of the earth world that are far from being devoid of colour; that on the contrary, they are so filled with colour as to be regarded as a veritable paradise in this respect. That is perfectly true, but even the most delectable regions of your terrestrial globe are dingy compared with the realms of light of the spirit world. The climate, you will affirm, has much to do with it. In these earthly paradises the weather as a rule is clement and the sunshine is lavish. That is equally true, but of them we are not speaking.

The realms of light teem with colour. The buildings, whether the great halls and temples or the simple and unobtrusive 'private' dwellings, are constructed of materials in which colour is always present. Even the paved ways are in colour. The trees, the flowers, the grass, the very soil in which these grow and thrive, the water, whether it be of sea, river or lake, are revelations of colour in every shade, blend, and tint.

Lastly, ourselves. Our spirit clothes are the very embodiment of colour for I verily believe that the widest variety and distribution of blends are to be perceived in our personal habiliments, reflecting, as they do, all the extremely fine gradations of spiritual progression. In this respect colour might serve the purpose of a recording instrument.

You have no scientific instrument on earth that could register results as accurately as colour registers the least degree of our spiritual progression for in this regard colour is *infallible* in what it reveals. There is no such thing as being able to assume a colour to which one is not entitled by reason of not having earned it. When you hear wise people on earth tell you that we who communicate are nothing but devils masquerading as 'angels of light', they are uttering the most blatant nonsense and displaying the most profound ignorance of common, elementary, spiritual laws.

Let me say this with emphasis: it is utterly *impossible for anyone* in the spirit world, no matter who it may be, to assume the tiniest, most minute spark of light to which he is not entitled. Light and colour mean spirituality; their absence, the lack of it. There are no exceptions, no deviations. That is a fundamental law operating throughout the entire spirit universe; a law that is fixed and immutable. Colour is natural to the realms of light. In the grey lands and the lands of darkness it is absent.

With us colour is light, and the light is living light. That, I admit, is difficult to follow, but it is capable of a little elucidation. In this way: take for example, your precious stones, and particularly the diamond. Now all precious stones on earth rely for their beauty upon external light. From the purely artistic point of view, all your precious stones become valueless when they are in absolute darkness. They might be composed of some common substance for all the worth they then are, but the instant they are brought into the light, either artificial or that of the sun, their lustre becomes immediately apparent. The stones are in that respect dead; they have no life in them for they contain no luminosity of their own, and are obliged to rely solely upon reflected or transmitted light.

We have a myriad forms of precious stones in these lands, and of such transcendental beauty and lustre as to surpass, beyond conception, anything that has ever been discovered, fashioned, or created upon earth. Every form of gem in turn has its wide range of colours, from the palest to the deepest. Diamond, emerald, sapphire, ruby, topaz, to name the most familiar to you, are all represented here, but every stone, no matter whether it be as small as the tip of your little finger or larger than your clenched hand, each single stone carries its own perfect light.

It gives forth its superb colours unaided for it needs no external source of illumination, either reflected or transmitted. It is itself alive. It glows and sheds its exquisite rays with incomparable, ineffable, splendour. The stones are flawless, *every one of them*. It is impossible to detect the most microscopic blemish upon any stone. Priceless, you will say. Indeed, they are for they are not to be bought. They can only be *earned*.

For use a personal adornment, these matchless and priceless jewels are given to us as part of our spiritual rewards. They constitute some of those wonderful adjuncts to our life here that bring joy not only to the possessors of them, but to all who behold them upon others. A little fanciful, you will perhaps hint, or eccentric. Not in the least. Were you able to take one of these gems in your hand, all your mundane ideas upon the subject would vanish upon the instant. Those of my earthly friends whose vision has been cultivated, and who are able to see such things as these, will readily be able to substantiate my words, if so be it they have actually seen jewels of the spirit world.

While I am upon the subject, the workmanship in the settings of our jewels is, of course, in perfect keeping with the lustrous stones. They are worn upon the person as part of a head-dress, or as fastening upon a girdle, or suspended from a chain round the neck. And so another chapter is added to the volume of colour.

As it is with our precious stones, so is it with the stones of lesser value—our building materials. The surface of your stone is dull and without colour. The purist will say I am wrong there because the earthly stone can be grey or cream, or even red in tone. Of course, but what of the rest of the colours of the spectrum? Where are those to be found in your stonework?

The surface of our stone—and you will understand that I am here using earthly terms to describe spirit-world substances—the surface of our stone has an alabaster-like translucence. Upon close examination, it is at once observed that the colour and the light which gives it life come from within the substance itself. It literally glows, yet it has not the appearance of being *illuminated* from within.

My present difficulty, you see, is to convey my meaning when I have nothing with which to draw a comparison for you because there is nothing upon earth akin to our building materials. The best I can do, therefore, is to try to set down what we see when we gaze about us, and to do so in as literal terms as possible.

The colour of the stone, then, shines forth, but you must not assume from this that all our buildings are aglitter with rays of coloured light, flashy and flamboyant. The glow that one perceives is a soft, gentle, delicate glow of subdued light, not a sharp, penetrating, flood of light, while the colours have the texture of pastel shades as you know them. As the buildings are set amid beautiful gardens with a wealth of flowers and trees and lawns, the colour of the edifice must accord with its environment and not, by the power of its vividness, overwhelm the hues of nature itself.

I must reaffirm that the shades of colour in our buildings are extremely delicate, so that when I tell you that we have such architectural glories as Gothic cathedrals, just as on earth (though used for a very different purpose), and that they are built in coloured stone, there is no occasion to take alarm when I suggest that you can emulate us in all the new buildings which in time will rise upon earth. The question of purple cathedrals does not arise! Nor of a flaring scarlet one either!

Once more I do not pretend to prophesy, but to mark for you a trend which is to be observed in our laboratories here, namely, that in due time a substance will be discovered or evolved—or invented if you wish— that will enable builders on earth to apply a surfacing to their buildings harder and more durable than at present known or used. Into this will be incorporated any colouring matter of whatever shade is desired from brilliant hard colours to delicate soft tints.

Of whatever the building itself may be constructed, this substance will be applied last of all, and give a most beautiful shade and texture to the whole fabric. It will be smooth and easily cleaned, but with the absence of smoke it will hardly become tarnished. That, my friends, is a simple forecast of what you should be able to do on earth if those 'in authority over you' will only bestir themselves, and think sometimes in terms of beauty and not merely of utility.

Why should you not have both beauty *and* utility in all your buildings? That is what we have in these highly serviceable lands of the spirit world. Just bethink you what a difference it would make in the whole appearance of your cities and towns were tasteful harmonious colour schemes to be introduced everywhere. In time your own homes will benefit as well for these new discoveries are meant for all people.

I have been permitted to peep into some of the laboratories here from time to time, and that is one item I am allowed to reveal to you. Not a very mighty one, you may say, but nevertheless one that should ultimately help to bring some of that urgently needed colour into the unutterable greyness of the earth—or some quarters of it.

I freely admit that when I was incarnate the old earth looked a very good place in which to live, and in those days I knew little or nothing—mostly nothing!—of what was to follow. I was contented to cling to my life on earth for as long as it was permitted, and to leave it with as good grace as possible. I hope I succeeded in accomplishing the latter. I rather fancy I did, for my friends of those days would say that I had a 'very good death', meaning, as far as they could see, a truly 'pious' one! We have had much laughter upon this subject since then.

However, the earth seemed a pleasant place, and I was not bothered about the colourlessness of it—until I came here. Then I saw just what I had left behind me as I perceived to what I had come. It is as though you were to gaze upon two pictures, the one in plain grey monochrome and the other in full colour. Try that simple little experiment for yourself, and then, my friends, you will have some idea—some *very small* idea—of the difference between the absence of colour in your world of the earth and the profusion of colour in our world of the spirit.

Mistaken Views

Views are varied among the incarnate as to the exact
spiritual position, or proper designation, of the realms
wherein I live. Some will regard them not as 'heaven'
itself, but as a kind of annexe thereto; an outland of
heaven rather than the place of celestial bliss which the
majority have in mind.

Such a conception arises, one imagines, from the fact
that in these lands we have so much (it might be
objected) of a very material nature, for what could be
more material than houses and buildings generally,
and gardens, and rivers and seas, not to mention our
multifarious occupations? Such things do not seem
concordant with one's idea of heaven.

No, they do not, but that is because the common idea
of heaven is built altogether upon wrong foundations.
The part of the spirit world, therefore, in which I live,
could be regarded as not being of the nature of heaven
at all. For heaven is unquestionably the abode of angels
and saints, and those beings could not, by any freak of
the imagination, be the least interested in, or concerned
with, such material things as I have recounted to you
as the grand features of these particular regions.

It is difficult to do other than associate heaven with
religion because the Church has always claimed
exclusively to deal with such matters as the 'soul's
salvation', and that closely concerns heaven, that most
difficult place to enter. What it really amounts to, then,

is that I—with countless others like me—am not in heaven at all, but decidedly outside it. We shall see about that later.

There is another view often expressed upon this subject, namely that while we may be immensely happy in these realms, yet we are hardly of a very spiritualised nature. As we go on progressing, we shall leave behind us this material order of life, and become highly etherealised. We shall proceed from realm to realm, ever higher and higher. Just so. Then what happens?

According to some of the incarnate, we shall become so spiritually elevated that we shall be forced to stay where we are, for to descend to a lower plane would mean the most exquisite torture to us. The 'physical' aspects of our bodies will similarly undergo a transmogrification until we lose all semblance of our former selves, as our many friends know us, and develop into beings (so it would appear) composed entirely of light, possessing very little real substance, hardly distinguishable from one another either in form or feature, and dispossessed of every human attribute, featureless, humourless and remote. Let me say emphatically that this is not so. Very far from it.

Who shall say where heaven begins? He would be a bold one among us here in these lands who would venture upon an answer. What are the facts? I can only give them to you *as I find them*, and that is as millions of others find them too. If you wish to say that these realms are of a material nature, then do so by all means. You will be affirming precisely the same as we do. We are eternally thankful that they *are* material. Everything is most gloriously solid round about us. Excellent! That is just as we like it.

The water is wet and sparklingly clear, the light is

bright and beautiful. The clothes we wear feel exquisite to the touch, and the chairs in which we sit are most commodious and comfortable. If we proceed to another realm we may find the water is thick and dirty, and the light *not so* bright. That, you will perhaps remark, is understandable. But what if we proceed in another direction? We shall observe that the water is still more sparklingly clear, the seating arrangements are even more commodious and comfortable than our own, and the light a great deal stronger and more beautiful. And so it will be all the way through the realms of light. The highest realms are every atom as material to the residents of those realms as are these realms to us. I might add that the high realms are as material to us of a *lower* realm, who are privileged to visit them, as are our own.

What of the beings who inhabit those lofty regions? Most certainly they are not mere masses of light and little else. Immense light they assuredly have, but that is part of their nature, not their whole form and substance. There are folk on earth who would declare that it is not possible to gaze upon one of these beings, and survive. That is pure nonsense.

We have all of us, at one time and another, gazed upon these personages for a measurable time, and we are still very much surviving. The three of us, Edwin, Ruth, and I, have visited a most illustrious being in his own surroundings. We have been shown parts of the realm in which he has his *home*—and I use the word in its literal sense. We were not obliged to shade our eyes in his presence to prevent any blaze of light from consuming us. We sat in very comfortable chairs in a superb apartment, whence we could look upon magnificent gardens. This great man spoke to us as we— and you—would expect any rational being to address us.

It was a breath-taking experience, of course, and one, moreover, which we have repeated upon numerous other occasions. Again, this same person has visited us in our own realm. He has even called upon us at our home, and seated himself in our chairs, and admired our house and all that it contains. He has graced us by his presence when we have had a social gathering of friends—artists and musicians, and the like. He has spoken to us then as a company, and to us individually upon our various efforts.

He has cheered and encouraged us with his words, and helped to resolve our difficulties. He has joined with us in these little assemblies without any suggestion, without the slightest hint even, that being in conditions so far removed from his own, he was undergoing a severe trial of spiritual endurance. There is not an individual *in these or in any other* of the realms of light who does not know him by sight, by voice, by illustrious fame. His visitations through all the realms are 'high days and festivals' with us, as he comes upon his 'official' journeyings.

When he visits us personally—and why should he not if such is his wish?—he cannot, of course, remain unnoticed by others, but the 'private' nature of his coming is accorded a ready appreciation. And what *he* can do, others of less spiritual altitude also are able to do—and they do it. In his transit, this great person has not lost any of the stupendous attributes which are his. He is not so etherealised as to be, to all appearances, a mass of light. He is human in these lower realms even as he is in his own natural environment. We have seen him in both places, and therefore we can speak from first hand experience.

As we progress and advance from realm to realm, we retain our individuality as well as the outward form and features by which we are recognised. The light which bespeaks our spiritual elevation may become more intense, but never so much as to submerge, beneath its power and brilliance, that which is our very personality. Certainly, to a person of low spirituality, the brightness of light would be blinding, but we are not inhabitants of those dark realms, and our eyes are not vexed by such light, but rather should we bask in the rays of spiritual greatness.

When we make visits to the higher realms some adjustment is necessarily made, but the latter is not to prevent us from being consumed or so bedazzled that our wits would desert us under the magnitude of spiritual splendour. Our personal feelings at what we see may be overwhelming, but that is induced by our sense of spiritual inferiority, by the perfection of what are beholding. Our hearts and minds may be full, but we suffer no bodily discomfort.

What do we see when we mount to these rarefied realms? According to most religious accounts, one can see nothing but some species of 'cloudy magnificence', and precious little else. Complete idleness would there seem to be the order of things except for an unremitting programme of hymn-singing, and an eternity of prayer and praise. What it comes to, then, in the minds of some folk, is that the higher one ascends spiritually the less one does actively, until the moment arrives when one does nothing at all but 'lift up the voice in song'.

What becomes of the accumulated knowledge and wisdom for which these high beings are renowned? Surely it is a shameful waste of such superlative attributes merely for the owners of them to devote their whole time to spiritual vocalistic exercises. And what a strange conception of the Father of the Universe to suppose that He should require such profitless services rendered to Him. That does not bespeak an all-wise Being.

Logic and sanity revolt at such an *outré* notion. It is not surprising, for logic and sanity are both right. No, my dear friends, the spirit world is conducted upon far better and more rational lines than that.

All our efforts in these lands of light are directed towards a *useful* purpose. Bear that always in mind. We aim to serve our fellows, whether incarnate or discarnate (as you would call us), usefully, and in serving you, we serve the Father of us all. And He wants us to do *useful* work; work that will bring some measure of good to some person. That rule—as one might name it—applies to all the realms of the spirit world, even to the highest.

You would be astonished at the colossal amount of work that goes on continuously in those high realms. There is no time to spare for the inordinate singing of 'spiritual Canticles'; there are far more important things to be done. I know at least one of these high personages to whom singing of this description would be positively unendurable. Not that we do not have the most beautiful voices in these lands. But the hymn, envisaged by so many of the incarnate, does not belong to the highest form of the musical art. Nor must it be thought that spiritual elevation brings with it, *ipso facto*, a superb singing voice.

The human voice can be very lovely, and, musically speaking, is really the most wonderful of all instruments, but fortunately for us all, we know how to use it in these lands—and when not to use it! Unfortunately for you, you have not as yet heard how truly beautiful good singing can be. Unless your psychic talents have been cultivated, you are not likely to— until you come here to reside.

So, as we progress into those high realms, we shall not lose our individuality in supposed etheric clouds, and become lost to everyone except the dwellers therein. We shall ever continue to be ourselves, our true selves: refined, to be sure, more etherealised, but still you will be you, and I shall be I—no one else. You and I will recognise each other, just as you will recognise all your friends, as they will recognise you.

In the immense future that lies before us we shall not become lost to the companions who are the joy of our lives. Some may advance along the road of progression a trifle faster than others, but we shall always be able to meet as of old. Our wisdom and knowledge will also increase. There will ever be a thousand good purposes to which to devote them.

The highest realms of the spirit world are no abodes of idleness; on the contrary, they are brim-full of useful activity.

'What becomes of our sense of humour when we pass into the spirit world?' is a question that will have occurred to many. It would seem that throughout the numerous communications that have come from us there has so far been no evidence of any humour at all. What is the reason for that, do you suppose? Let me hasten to affirm that whatever sense of humour we may have possessed on earth is fully retained when we pass into the spirit world.

It is a strange thing that among the cardinal virtues that have been catalogued, enumerated, dissected, and enlarged upon by sundry Fathers of the Church, as well as written about by later church men, with copious annotations thereupon, no mention has been made of a sense of humour, not so much as by oblique reference. It is not even to be found included among the 'deadly sins'. Why this omission, one wonders ? Certainly one does come across allusions to 'holy mirth', whatever that may be. It rather points to the kind of ecclesiastical frivolity that one would meet at parochial garden parties, of which I have a lively recollection from my incarnate days!—that is, humour of a very restrained 'pious' order.

Though there is much that occurs upon earth that can, and does, cause deep sadness in our hearts, yet there is also much that gives us occasion for laughter in the spirit world. We can derive amusement from some of the 'wisdom' of the incarnate.

There are scientific gentlemen and great philosophers on earth whose knowledge and talents have gained them almost world-wide renown. Such is the habit of the incarnate that folk of this kind are regarded as the repository of most of the wisdom. Consequently, their views are asked upon every subject under the earthly sun; however far beyond the orbit of their knowledge and experience, it matters not.

Not infrequently, some of these gentlemen will dignify the columns of some journal with the fruits of their wisdom. Sooner or later they are bound to be asked if they believe in a 'hereafter', and if so, is it possible to communicate with the denizens of the unseen world? How often is the answer: No, I do not believe a next world exists for the simple reason that no one has ever come back from it to tell us so.

Such an answer as that, my dear friends, can shake the spirit world, and cause whole realms to roar. For we can see the truly funny side of such a portentous declaration, and assess the speaker's worth at its true evaluation. For the living millions of us here to be pronounced upon as non-existent by one individual, upon whom so much reliance is placed by earth folk, does really have its humorous aspect. At least, that is how we can regard it, though at the same time lament the display and dissemination of such arrant nonsense.

The scientists and philosophers of the earth are not entirely unknown to us here. Naturally, if any one of them shows the least glimmering of perceiving the truth of the reality of the spirit world, we are anxious to bring that man forward as much as we are able, so that by adequate investigation and research he may become a spiritual beacon, as it were, for the incarnate. So much weight is attached to the words that fall from the mouths of the famous upon earth that it is not only a matter of the truth, but of who speak that truth.

It is peculiar that a sense of humour is a subject that has always been omitted from all religious thought and deliberations. It is as though humour of any sort belongs exclusively to the earth, and that with the death of the physical body all sense of humour is halted at the very portal of the spirit world, there to be cast off and abandoned for ever. There could be no greater mistake than to suppose anything of the sort.

If a sense of humour is part of our natural composition on earth, then we shall take it with us to the spirit world at our dissolution and we shall find plenty of means and opportunity to indulge it. Religion, of one kind or another, being so inseparably bound up in the minds of earth people with 'life after death', it is not to be contemplated for one moment that humour can possibly enter into the scheme of heavenly things in the minutest degree. That would be a degradation of all that is supposedly holy. At most, there might be that 'holy mirth' to which I have alluded.

Pictures that show angels robed in shimmering white garments, embarrassed with enormous wings and with faces displaying no known emotion whatsoever, have given to the world an entirely false notion. Even the term 'angels and saints' is spiritually forbidding, and robs exalted personages of all their intense humanity and warmth of feeling, substituting a remote, cold, bleak spirituality.

You will read here and there in the communications that have come from us how that we hear the sounds of merry laughter going on round about us. Something must have caused that laughter for we are not so empty-headed that we laugh at nothing. We are not given to hysterical fits and outbursts. No, our laughter is genuine because it has a genuine cause. We have much that we *can* laugh at, and not least among commonplace subjects is *ourselves*. That is something which, very early in our lives in these lands, we can learn to do. Here is the realisation of the poet's wish that we could see ourselves as others see us. In doing so, if we have a nicely developed sense of humour, we find an ample field for the expression of it.

What form does our humour take? That, I am afraid, is a question that it is virtually impossible to answer for the same reason that you would find it impossible to describe to the dweller of another world what it is that provokes your mirth. Humour is a mental disposition; the causes that give rise to it can be fugitive in the extreme. There is this one can say: oftentimes the people of earth provide us with somewhat to laugh at, when, in all earnestness and seriousness, they make statements concerning us of the spirit world which, though seemingly of deep significance to you, are to us decidedly amusing.

Here is an example. It is customary, among those who know us and speak with us regularly and naturally, to designate our spiritual status or quality by referring to our particular 'vibrations'. If we are of some spiritual elevation we become people of 'high vibration', while the reverse is the case, people from the low realms being of 'low vibration'. The very process and proceedings of communication will also be upon a 'high' or 'low' vibration, according to circumstances.

To refer to some illustrious soul from the highest realms of the spirit world as of a 'high vibration' strikes us as a quaint mixture of the quasi-scientific with the purely unimaginative. It is a method of spiritual appraisement which we never use, nor even think of, during our intercourse with one another in these lands. Though it may answer its purpose in a way, and serve to convey some sort of idea, yet it is most uncomplimentary, to say the least.

It is, in fact, a trifle too 'scientific' so that a most wonderful personality becomes entirely lost—or overlooked, shall I say?—in the anxiety to estimate that person's number of 'vibrations per second'. I have purposely put that baldly—but I hope not unkindly—because I am anxious to show you that we do not distinguish each other's spiritual quality upon a vibrational basis any more than do you of each other.

In your normal intercourse upon earth you do not ask, 'Is so-and-so a pleasant person?'—and have for reply: 'Oh, yes; charming. High vibration!' At least, not if you are normally constituted.

Let us examine the matter a little more closely. High and low vibrations are taken as meaning of high spirituality on the one hand, and of low spirituality on the other. In fact, good and bad. The higher they are the more spiritual; the lower the less spiritual.

But what happens when the vibrational computations are transferred to musical sound? As you will perhaps know, musical instruments are rendered in tune with one another by adopting a certain note as standard pitch. From that single note, all others of the scale are brought into complete attunement. The note so used is measured by its number of vibrations per second. The higher the note, the greater the number of vibrations.

A note in *altissimo* will be of a high vibration. As we descend the scale the vibrations become slower, or fewer or lower—until we have the deep rich bass notes, which are so indispensable to music generally. Here is a question for you to answer. If a high vibration means *high* spirituality and a low vibration means low spirituality, is a high note therefore *good* and a low note therefore *bad*? There surely must be some relationship between a person who vibrates at a very slow rate, and a musical note that does the same thing.

Yet what could be nicer than the full notes of a deep bass singer? We mostly like those notes, and wonder just how far down the scale the singer can really descend! What about all the bass instruments of the orchestra, so vitally necessary in music? Are they essentially *bad* in some way or another? If so, it would seem deplorably bad fortune upon the players of them. To be compelled to play upon an instrument of low vibration would appear to be a most inhuman state of affairs, and one that should have instant attention with a view to its quick abolition. Where, too, would the organ be without its profound pedal notes? The music would be incomplete without it, and would sound top-heavy.

Music notes are measured by their cycles, their vibrations per second. It is a satisfactory method of obtaining unity of tuning. But on earth measurement by vibrations is mostly confined to musical sounds. It is such a pity that it has been adopted to measure our spiritual stature in the spirit world. I think we are worthy of something better, something more dignified, more friendly and affectionate, and more truthful. It is as though you had your fingers upon our spiritual pulse just in the same way as your doctor takes your physical pulse to learn how it is with you, medically speaking. If the pulse is beating its correct number, all is well—a good vibration!

Well, well, my friends, we need not take this matter too seriously. If you can see the pleasant side of it, perhaps the funny side of it, then take it as evidence that I have not completely lost my sense of humour since I came to dwell here. Though it may not be humour of a high order (high vibration?) if it has brought a smile to your face in these harassing times upon earth, so much the better and perhaps I shall, in this instance, have deserved well of you.

I am reminded of a contemporary of mine, a preacher of great renown, and extremely popular. His popularity was founded upon—or gained by—an unusual phenomenon. At some moment during his sermons he invariably managed to make his congregation laugh. It was not, of course, hilarious laughter, being tempered both to the place and the occasion, but laughter it unmistakably was.

This was regarded as something so out of the ordinary that his fame soon spread. It never seemed to bring anything in the way of ecclesiastical censure, the large congregation that he drew possibly acting as a palliative, and the priest and his people went upon their ways that much the happier. And why not, pray? Why should laughter be so rigorously banned or excluded from religion?

The truth is that organised religion needs to relax the tension to which it has submitted its followers. Churchgoing has developed into a grim business. There is little warmth in the services and less of truth in what is disseminated from the pulpit, though of the latter we will not speak just now. Humour is no sin. Laughter of the right kind is one of the best things on earth—or in heaven—for man. Alas, that there is so little of it upon earth at these times for folk are feeling the great strain of past distresses and pains and of present frustrations.

But lightness of heart *will* return to our friends on earth. Without anticipating what I have to say later on here, you must not suppose that we are insensible to the dreadful storm of sadness and trouble through which the earth has passed. So much of both have inevitably been brought into these lands. Inasmuch as folk have reached a safe harbour when they have at last travelled into these realms at their earthly journey's end, so have we used our best methods of bringing back to sorrowful souls a full measure of the true joy of living, of which the bestialities of the earth had deprived them.

Folk who for years had forgotten what it was even to smile have again found themselves with their hearts warmed and their minds comforted and raised up, and by and by they have discovered that their sense of humour, which they thought had forever been beaten down, has returned to them in full vigour. I venture to say, in good truth, that the *heavenly* laughter which they heard, engendered by real human beings and begotten of kindness and joy of heart, did what no stern cold religion could ever do.

Such folk were not interested in the generally accepted notion of angels, the conventional type of frigid spirituality, but they found that the free and friendly ministrations of kind and loving souls were an expression of humanity at its highest level.

Many times have we laughed, in the greatest good humour, with illustrious souls from the highest realms, and there need be no doubt that if they can and do laugh, then it is no 'high crime and misdemeanour' for us infinitely lesser folk to do the same. But we cannot always bring our laughter with us when we come to speak with you on earth. We must be very sure of our audience first because of the mistaken notion that laughter and spirituality cannot go hand in hand.

It is a pity that such an erroneous idea has taken root, but there it is. If some of us were to introduce that which would make you laugh we should, most likely, be branded as low, frivolous people with whom it were better not to have any intercourse.

Amongst our own special friends who know us well, and whom we know well, the case is a little different. But for general purposes, the rule is that we should not exhibit anything that might be mistaken for levity. Hence it is that the query arises as to our sense of humour. Seriousness has its proper place, I need hardly say, and we should never go beyond what good sense suggests and proper taste orders.

As things are at present, we must suffer the unmerited reputation of being a humourless body of people, with no sense of what is harmlessly amusing. If we speak with a lightness that is natural to an ordinary human being—and there are human beings in the highest regions of the spirit world!—our words will be condemned as trivial rubbish. However sublime the truth we may tell, yet if it be not framed elegantly and display great rhetorical qualities, and be not declaimed with a voice from which every trace of honest friendliness has been expunged in favour of the oratorical, then it is said that nothing ever came from the spirit world that was not upon an extremely low and paltry level.

People do not want us as we are, but as they think we ought to be, and that imposes something of a strain upon some of us—indeed, upon many of us. We want to be our normal selves. We do not wish to affect a tone of voice or a form of demeanour that is foreign to us. We love to laugh. We have ample time in which to be serious just as have you. We can give forth our literature when the occasion demands, though there are many who deny that sternly.

We may have these arbitrary limitations imposed upon us, but when you at length come to this world of the spirit, you will be deeply thankful to perceive that laughter is not only permitted but encouraged, and that in coming to us here you have brought with you your sense of humour. Never fear, you will have plenty of opportunities to exercise it.

Beauty

If more colour is wanted upon earth, as I suggested to you earlier, more beauty is also greatly needed.

There was a time when men covered themselves with woad. Whether this was done to frighten their enemies, or to repel malevolent spirits, or merely to pleasure their friends, it is of no consequence. What does matter is that colour came to be introduced into the life of early man. It was a step in the right direction.

When primitive man, as he is called, made his scratchy drawings upon the walls of his caves, the first attempts at self-expression through the art of drawing, that, too, was a move in the right direction. How far has the earth world advanced since those very distant days? It has progressed much in purely material things, and at a fairly rapid pace. But spiritually? That is another story.

The earth has never been 'out of touch' with the spirit world. In those far off times inspiration of one kind and another came to the earth with regularity. The wise beings of the highest realms have been and are always responsible for sending to the earth those 'telementations', as such transmission of thought has been named, to be used for the benefit and betterment of man. It needs not to tell you that they have not always been so employed.

The steady improvement has gone on. Just cast your mind back, and bethink you of the great changes that have come about from those early days. There, in the past, would be thousands of people passing into the spirit world from ailments and diseases which, to your modern notions, would seem strange because, although still to be suffered today, yet has medical science made such enormous strides that the doctors can quickly relieve the afflicted and effect a cure, you would say, almost overnight, where your ancestors would have perished miserably.

Yes, indeed, material progress has been great and good, but while man upon the one hand has laboured through medical research to preserve and prolong the life of his fellows, on the other he has perverted his 'discoveries' which is another way of indicating his inspiration—to the destruction of man by turning his knowledge to the making of lethal weapons of vast explosive power, where the victims can be numbered in their hundreds of thousands—and in the aggregate, millions—of souls. So spiritual progress has been checked and overwhelmed by this 'good' material progress. That is one instance, but it is by far the worst. The remainder are inconsiderable beside it.

If you were able to glance at some regions of the earth as they were in days gone past, you would be struck by their greater beauty as compared with what you are able to observe now. The people were clothed in colourful garments of a picturesque kind and the style of architecture was delightful to look upon, albeit there were many black patches in every town—a state of affairs not entirely unheard of *now*.

In the inspiration that comes from the spirit world, the whole emphasis is always and must always be upon *beauty*, where it concerns what we all call the fine arts. The painters of old did what they could according to their limitations. For the painter, in common with the sculptor, the musician, and the like, had to begin somewhere. He was not born such. From the initial tentative scrawls on the walls of the caves he had to be gently led inspirationally into deeper and broader channels.

It must not be thought that inspiration is given only to the pious and holy, the ascetic, the recluse or the dreamer. Inspiration is transmitted from the spirit world to the earth where it has best chance of being perceived, accepted and acted upon in the true and right direction. It would be something of waste of time and endeavour to try to give spiritual teachings to a man who was a religious bigot, so confirmed in his bigotry that nothing would move him from his stubbornness of thought, and who moreover, held the belief that all 'spirits who manifested' in whatever way were 'devils in disguise'. A far better spot than that could assuredly be found for the gentle instillation of the truths of the spirit world.

The early painter, then, did earnestly and energetically his true best to paint *what he really saw*. His achievement often fell short of his ambition and his strivings, but he continued to labour, often-times with inferior materials, continued to perceive the promptings from the spirit world, and with such at his elbow, as it were, he progressed from the more or less crude and untrue-to-life to the more advanced and true-to-life.

If so be it you should ever cast your eyes upon the paintings of the ancient masters, perhaps you would, of your kindness and charity, call to mind what I have just been discussing with you, and condemn not those master painters of the past. For what they did, they did in all honesty of purpose and from motives that were spiritually lofty. They were as yet unskilled, their materials were poor and often lacking. All those painters are now in the spirit world, and the quality of their present work is as far removed from their early incarnate efforts as light is from darkness.

The same thing applies to so many other departments of human endeavour. But the tendency has been to deviate from the path it was best to follow, and to pursue other and less attractive avenues, simply because man is at liberty to exercise his free will. He gets a trifle out of hand at times, a thought wilful, and eager to go upon his own. That is how it is viewed in the spirit world. It is not so much a retrogressive step, as a side-step. The temptation has been to become more ornate, as you will see in art, in architecture, and music, for example.

As time passed, still greater changes were made until, arriving at the present day, the hideous is enthroned, the cult of the ugly has been initiated. What could be more ugly than the earth's barrack-like buildings, set four-square, unrelieved by the slightest ornament, and displaying rows of apertures—the window openings?

Music composed in what is known as the 'modern' idiom is barbaric, and the art of painting has degenerated in many quarters into nightmarish daubs of pure puerility while drawings are often in imitation of the unskilled efforts of the novice. How does this come about? Where is the inspiration?

According to what I have just said, these craftsmen are inspired from the spirit world. That is perfectly true, and the statement still stands. Inspiration can come from every conceivable part of the spirit world, high or low, light or dark. All the dreadful art forms are inspired by the lower realms, *and nowhere else.* What man chooses to do of his own volition does not alter the case. If he elects to debase his art, his debased spirit inspirers will rejoice. On the other hand, if he should decide to listen only to those lofty beings of the highest realms his art will be as pure as he is able to make it. For there is a vast difference between that which is poorly executed for lack of means, knowledge, and proficiency, and that which is a deliberate and successful attempt to depict what is obscene, artistically speaking.

You may query how it is possible that such frightful art forms should receive any encouragement whatever from your fellows incarnate. The answer, as we in the spirit world see it, lies in the fact that folk are not honest with themselves. No one will know of such dishonesty for their reasons or their motives will remain secret for just so long as they wish them to be. It is very different in the spirit world. Here our motives have their immediate effect, and men must be honest with themselves for they cannot evade being so. It is useless to pose and pretend; no one will be deceived by shams and falsities. With you it is otherwise, hence your debased arts.

There are also vanity and conceit to be considered. There are folk who like to adopt or patronise a new form of art as something extraordinary which, by virtue of their superior minds, they are able to comprehend and appreciate, and disclose hidden beauties that lesser people cannot perceive. It is in every sense a hoax. Unhappily, it is accepted in the higher places in response to a supposed 'popular demand'.

In music, these 'authorities' will say, one never knows when and where a genius may be lurking. Consider the experiences of the past where a composer has been condemned ruthlessly by his contemporaries, only to be hailed with delight and acclaim as a master by later generations. We must not throw away any chance (the authority will add) that presents itself of discovering and fostering a potential genius. The public must hear this work, if it be music; or enabled to view it, if it be a painting. The public shall be the judge. Thus does authority delude itself—and the people of earth. Such a state of affairs does not and cannot exist in these lands—for which we are eternally thankful.

The aim of these mockeries of artists, they will themselves claim, is to find a new medium of expression, or utilising the old medium, to find new art forms. That is the claim, and the result is an abomination. It takes a real genius to discover a new art form, and these small people are far from being that. New art forms are the direct inspiration of the spirit world. They will be sent *only* when the *authorities* of the spirit world deem it fit and proper to do so. The instruments through whom they will present to the earth any new form will have been examined and tested first.

Then how are you to know what is a new art form, and that it derives from the right quarters? You will know, my friends, by one simple test—its beauty. The earth world is no longer fundamentally primitive in the arts, though it may be extraordinarily primitive in other respects, its method of settling international arguments and disagreements, for example.

History reveals the different epochs through which music, for instance, has passed, and it is not difficult to place one's finger upon the real geniuses who have helped music upon its way. The same thing applies to painting. You will understand, of course, that when I speak of inspiration I do not mean that every wretched, ugly, tinkling little piece of so-called music, and every horrid little daub, are works of evil inspiration. There is much imitation goes on in such cases for the cult of the unpleasant attracts other empty minds.

There it is, you will remind me: the earth is free and nothing can be done about it. So is the spirit world free, much freer than ever the earth world could be, but we manage somehow!—as no doubt you will have gathered by now. Once more, let us not take things too seriously, by which I mean, we need not distress ourselves unduly. We might with complete justification bring whatever sense of humour we have to bear upon the case, a course of action I heartily recommend to your notice.

You can be sure of this: the masterpieces will live, the travesties of art will perish. If these so-called artists and composers could be accorded the ridicule they justly deserve, if they were not taken so seriously, which flatters their silly vanity and encourages them to perpetrate more artistic horrors, they would soon cease to trouble the earth, and that would in turn save us some measure of trouble when they at length arrive in the spirit world.

Those 'artists' and 'composers' who have been deluded into a belief in their striking powers and unmatched genius, and who come here with their absurd notions and self-delusions fast upon them, have the shock of their lives when the great awakening comes upon them. Thinking themselves to be wonderful upholders of all that is beautiful in art, and believing themselves to be divine instruments for the creation of all that is noble, they discover that in place of being men of artistic substance they are men of artistic straw.

They see also that their work has no place in the spirit world, where absolute beauty is pre-eminent in the realms of light. The artist will soon learn that we do not have in these lands trees with purple trunks, yellow branches, and blue leaves, nor any other like distortions of nature. They must paint things here as they see them, *as they are*, and not as a disordered fancy takes them, nor a silly sham leads them to perpetrate.

The musician, too, if he be a real musician, will quickly apprehend that his earthly musical monstrosities will have no countenance here for a single instant. He will have to learn that his music must conform to certain natural laws, and that while he must not deviate from them, yet his range of invention is seemingly illimitable—at least, *his* genius is hardly likely to reach music's inventive boundaries. He, too, will realise that the laws of music are also the laws of beauty. No dreadful jangling prolongation of soul-disturbing discords, no series of unrelated notes and intervals denominated a melody, no fantastic disposition of instrumental playing that has not the advantage or quality of being really amusing nor the inherent skill of being clever. None of these barbarities is allowed to pose as music in these realms.

When we come to view the earth as a whole, without delving too deeply into such particular subjects as the arts, we can see how really ugly the earth can be. In nothing more so than in your very style of architecture is this so readily apparent. In this respect there has been retrogression. It might be said in extenuation that the needs of the case have had an adverse influence upon domestic architecture.

Populations have increased enormously beyond what they were so many hundreds of years agone. Consequently, living space has become more precious so that every available inch of it must be used to the greatest advantage. Hence the long dreary rows of ugly private dwellings, each jammed tight and close upon its neighbour, each mathematically similar, uninspiring, and *uninspired*. Colourless, grey, or just plain dirty.

It is scarcely wonderful when an inhabitant of one of those obnoxious dwellings comes to these realms that he or she—casting his eyes about him upon the glories and delights that surround him, should believe himself to have attained to the highest heaven of all. The transition from ugliness to pure beauty is violent in such cases, but the 'violence' is enjoyed to the full.

Now, we realise perfectly all your difficulties upon earth, not the least of them that of space. But what attempt has been made really to overcome them? Precious little, that is obvious. Your 'properly constituted authority', being something of a 'movable feast', you are never to know just exactly what you will get next. There are too many different opinions among them and not enough unity of purpose based upon ideas that will reveal in their achievement a perfect compound and balance of *usefulness and beauty*—the art of tectonics.

It is an art that has been almost lost. In your present days utility so often connotes bareness, frigid severity, unrelieved by a trace of colour. These, when added together, do not produce a total sum of beauty. Beauty of form has been sacrificed to strict utility. Individual craftsmanship has given way to production by the million. That has certain advantages because by it so many can partake of improvements, who would otherwise be debarred by expense. If it brings more brightness into more homes, then so much the better.

But there is this to be said. My informants of other days, who are also dwellers in these realms, tell me that in their day they combined usefulness and beauty in their work as a matter of course. The rule then was *beautify somehow* wherever possible. A small ornament tastefully executed was better than none at all. Improvements, they were advised, should always be considered in terms of what was pleasing to the eye, and all necessities should be similarly regarded. The craftsman, therefore, went upon his way as an individual who took a personal delight in his work because he knew that he would be identified with the result and not treated like a machine.

Material advancement on earth has meant the great building up of commerce, which is the chief concern of the towns and cities. It would be superfluous for me to recount to you what you will see in them. When you come to view our great cities of the spirit world you will see there no shops, no printed signs, none of the familiar indications of commerce, for of commerce we have none. Nor do we have such monsters of ugliness, factories. To build a beautiful earth in those regions that require it most should be the aim of those in whose hands is the government of the incarnate.

I have spoken to you of the way in which builders of olden time combined usefulness with beauty, and that in overcoming faults or defects they always were mindful of what was attractive to the eye. In my old house on earth there was a good deal of panelling. It was very lovely, and brought me much joy. But it also served a most useful purpose. It helped to make the apartments warm.

There was a time on earth when men began to build their dwellings a little more solidly by making them of stone. But they found in winter that the stone was cold and chilled the rooms. Even though doors and windows were adequately sealed, yet there still persisted cold draughts whose point of emergence seemed a mystery. The cold stone wall was the culprit. By the simple device of hanging material upon the walls and thus confining the cold surface, the unpleasant draughts were reduced.

In the larger houses, tapestries were freely introduced, just as I have tapestries in my home here, though for a very different reason. The art of the weaver was requisitioned to provide what was needful, and the fine arts were combined with strict utility. In some houses wood panelling was used to cover the walls. While it was excellent in itself, yet the carver was set to work to spread his art upon its surface, with what results most of you will be acquainted. It may have made the rooms somewhat dark after the sun had set, but what matter. Folk retired to their beds earlier in those days.

With my house on earth, I had the advantage of modern invention, and with its aid I still further improved upon the splendid work of those ancient artificers for I was able to light the chambers as strongly as I pleased, and so suffered no inconvenience from the darkness of the wood. I reaped enormous benefit to my personal comfort, both of body and mind, for the chill draughts were appreciably reduced, and the eye ever delighted in the lustre of the ancient panelling.

This is a small incident, of course; I recount it solely for your interest, and to point to the fact that through the ages the earth has never been without its inspired help in every shape and form, even to helping in making your earthly domicile a more fitting and comfortable place. To point, also, to the fact that all material advantages are not upon the exact lines which those of the highest realms had urged. The combination of the beautiful with what is useful has generally departed, and, indeed, often the useful is missing as well!

Even after usefulness has no further application, there is no reason why the beautiful should be abandoned in favour of the ugly. With such lovely things to choose from in this spirit world, yet I elected to retain the panelling upon my walls, simply because it is delightful. We have no chill draughts to combat here, but the wood-work—that is, the spirit world equivalent of wood-work—loses none of its beauty on that account. The panelling is serving a most useful purpose, and no one would wish to have it removed.

Service

At the commencement of the catechism, which I had occasion to use when I was incarnate, the answer to the question as to why God made us is that He did so 'to know Him, love Him, and serve Him in this world, and to be happy with Him for ever in the next.' Which is all very good, *as far as it goes*.

But it omits one very important point. The answer is explicit in declaring that we must serve God on earth, but it makes no mention of serving Him afterwards in the spirit world. Such service would appear to be confined to the earth, which would point to a life spent in complete idleness in the 'hereafter'.

Many would say that the 'life after death' will be devoted to concentrated efforts of 'praise and prayer' until weariness from this pursuit finally sets in, it is to be presumed, whereupon, it must be supposed further, that there remains nothing whatever to do but be happy, though how the latter is to be achieved no one could possibly know or even try to guess. We should be happy, and that was enough.

Doubtless some provision had been made that would ensure our happiness. Perhaps the mere state of being 'holy' would itself be the highest form of felicity, or to be in the permanent company of angels and saints would afford us unalloyed joy, especially if one engaged in pleasant theological or 'pious' discourse upon lines, of course, in strict keeping with the true Church to which we formerly belonged upon earth. This would raise extremely knotty problems because of the difficulty of ascertaining which of the hundreds of Churches is the true one beyond peradventure.

Or perhaps there would be a blending of them all, which in turn might raise further troubles for if none of the Churches can agree in their various doctrines on earth, is it to be expected that they will do so in heaven? The man who is accustomed to elaborate ritual and complicated doctrines might be revolted to think that heaven should also harbour a member of a church which regarded all ritual as rank superstition and complicated doctrines as devilish.

Between these two widely divergent types of religious thought and practice, there are countless other homemade religions, each claiming some portion of heaven as its own, if not the whole of it, and by something more than implication, ruthlessly debarring the members of all other denominations from even a small corner of the celestial realms. All of which, you will agree, makes things very awkward and difficult.

As the catechism makes no positive mention of anything to do in heaven, it seems impossible to think otherwise than that some very major complications must inevitably arise. It would not be proper to suggest that the devil always finds something for idle hands to do, for, after all, we are discussing heaven!

How near is that simple catechism answer to the truth—and how remotely far! For no one could quarrel with the first part of the answer as it deals with the earth world. It is when it ventures upon the second part that it gets 'all abroad and everywhere' but in the right spot.

Here is a simple question which might well be placed in the catechism: How is God best served by man? And here, too, is the answer in catechism style: God is best served by man when man serves his fellows.

The key-note of the spirit world, my friends, if I may so express it, is service. By service, I do not mean servitude for that is the last word to be applied to our service in these lands. Rather is it a word *never* to be applied.

Service is a term that covers an immensity of activities, occupations, endeavours and achievements. By service, we gain those many rewards which are here for the gaining. By it we gain our spiritual progression. Service is not comprised under any one heading. It is here and everywhere. There is no good thing we can do but that it will bring some good to some one. Often have I spoken to you of the work in these realms, and even attempted to give you some small account of our occupations and recreations. Work with us means service, not toil. It brings tangible results. We cannot buy service nor are we paid for it. We have no money nor its equivalent.

'Now it is all very well for you,' I hear you exclaim; 'you are not living in a world where, without money or something to take its place, you cannot survive. You do not have to work for a *living*, and by all accounts if you did nothing whatever, but remained utterly idle, you would not starve or go in rags.'

Perfectly true, my friends. You are living in a material world—so are we, if it comes to that. By material, of course, is meant a solid sort of world like the earth. Firm to the touch and real—above all things real. Precisely; that is just what our world of the spirit is—solid and real. Material, in fact, if anything can be. But we need not argue over terms.

Our world is as yet intangible to you—in the same way as yours is now to us, for we can comfortably walk through the thickest wall that was ever constructed on earth as though it had no existence, *which it has not for us, beyond a vague mistiness.*

Relatively, we are in a similar position to each other. Strange, is it not? You are vapoury to us, but solid to yourselves. We are vapoury to you, but solid to ourselves. So that we can both claim a share in the use of the word material in reference to our respective existences, your *temporary* one, and our *permanent* one. And if I might be allowed to voice a preference, I prefer the permanent one! I have yet to meet anyone who wishes he was back again upon the old earth.

Hundreds of years of orthodox religious teachings have implanted totally erroneous notions in the minds of incarnate men concerning the 'life after death'. What information does the Church possess about the spirit world? None. Its bolder members try their hand at speculation, but the fruits of their cogitations amount to precious little.

Death of the physical body has itself been made into a grim ogre by the thought of the 'great unknown' that is to follow it. A dreadful journey (it is always deemed) has to be undertaken. Artists and writers alike have combined to make the whole performance shocking, a horrifying business, whose outcome is unpredictable. Death, Judgement, Heaven or Hell, says the Church. That is the prospect before every soul. The first two are certain; there is no possibility of avoiding them. The next two—Heaven or Hell—it rests with man which he will choose. So proclaims the Church.

Life on earth is spent with that one dismal and awful end in view. Some folk elect to ignore the whole thing, preferring to wait with complete indifference, so they aver, for whatever may betide. Whether they actually do or not is a matter upon which some of us here could throw a little light. Others are so haunted by the thought of their last day on earth as to make their lives a misery to them. Others, again, have wrapped the spirit world in so many mysteries and strange beliefs as to make it a place hardly worth coming to—if it could be avoided—by virtue of the fact that those same beliefs have made of it the abode of mystic cranks.

They would have you believe that life here is one continual struggle of the soul to do something or other. It is never clearly defined precisely what. By the achievement of this intangible something, or by the imposition of remarkable but inexplicable 'tests', the soul is 'purged', while in the meantime, the victim is witnessing a variety of the oddest symbology that could find no place in the scheme of things here. That is dreadfully vague, but then so are the original concepts.

Eastern religions have contributed much to the formulation of a multitude of fantastic ideas relative to these beautiful lands in which I live. Such notions may suit the eastern mind, but they do not bear transplanting into other climes. The spirit world is a *practical* world, and its methods are business-like. Why should they not be? The earth people pride themselves upon such methods because it makes for efficiency. We, too, are efficient—highly efficient, far more so than you can ever be on earth, because we have far less restrictions both of body and mind. Our restrictions—if one can truthfully so designate them—simply mean that we obey the natural laws of these lands. They are not legal enactments imposed by the will of man.

I have witnessed the arrival in these lands of people whose numbers I cannot count, comprising folk from every walk of terrestrial life. I have witnessed the wide variety of emotions which they have exhibited upon the realisation of what has taken place in their lives. But never have I come across a soul who wished to go immediately into deep learned discourses about the soul, what it is, and how it functions.

Distress of mind, sorrow and anguish, remorse, the commonplace mental disturbances consequent upon seeing the truth at last, will naturally have their effect upon the new arrival. But we rigidly debar anything that is not severely practical in our service to such folk. Where possible, we calm the mind through the eye, by showing them the *kind* of place to which they have come. That usually answers the purpose. There is more to be learnt in the sight of a magnificent landscape than in a hundred homilies upon obscure mental processes as they are supposed to exist in the spirit world. That is part of our service, such service as the catechism fails to mention.

That small volume would lead you to infer that you are left to look after yourself on arrival here, except you be bound for the highest heaven among the angels and saints, where doubtless a reception committee would have everything properly in hand to welcome you, and add your name to the roll of the elect. You would, of course, need nothing else. No service of any sort.

In a short space of time, you would have left all your natural and customary environment amid your relatives and friends, left your earthly pursuits, and with the utmost precipitation landed among an enormous company of rarefied beings, and feeling yourself just like a fish out of water! You would do nothing because there is nothing to do, and your earthly spiritual mentors would say that you are in eternal bliss with everlasting happiness. Most likely you would feel thoroughly wretched, and question the happiness.

And you would be right. It is easy for some minds to decide wherein another's happiness shall rest. It is usually based upon their own predilections or tastes. Even we, in this land of clear perceptions, are not presumptuous enough to declare to folk what shall be their happiness. If we know their likes and wishes, we can guide and advise them in what manner they can be indulged, and thus they can attain their own true happiness. But in no case are we deciding for them or pronouncing upon what shall be their happiness.

It is said this world of the spirit is governed by thought, that thought is paramount. It is sometimes called a thought-world. Remembering how impalpable thought may seem to be, folk have not unnaturally believed us to be living in something akin to a dream state, where nothing is concrete, and which, as likely as not, is liable to fade into nothingness just as earthly dreams dissolve. All other things are consonant with that conception. We are 'shades'. Shades, indeed! Such people do not realise that it is they who are the weaker for their thoughts have no power in a creative sense on earth until they are translated into material form. With us our thoughts produce an immediate effect for we have no earthly state to interpose itself between our thought and its direct action. When we build, we build *more solidly* than you can ever hope to do on earth—and permanently. We have no tedious and protracted processes to undertake before our thoughts can have their full realisation.

I need not point to the immense shortages of necessary things from which you are suffering at this moment throughout so wide an area of the earth-plane. Such a condition could not exist here. Our building material for everything is thought, a never-failing substance which is durable and imperishable—until we have no further use for whatever it is we have created. We use our thoughts in service because, once again, there is no intervening earthly state to prevent their quick and direct action.

No, we are not shadows, wandering about in a wispy sort of way with nothing to do. We are intensely active, using our minds, producing concrete results in the service of our fellows. We do not have unbearable delays brought about by the petty minds of the inefficient. Nor do we have cranks trying to impose their wild, fallacious ideas upon us. *That* is not service as we know it.

Our work goes on because there is nothing to hinder its progress. We have no quarrels or disputes. We have no stoppages. And well for the people of earth it undoubtedly is that we do not, for their influence would be felt at once. We have no need here to belong to societies to secure our rights, or to redress our wrongs. Societies of that kind, in fact, do not exist. We depend upon each other *as do you*, did you but realise it fully.

With us service does not mean an eternal round of distasteful and laborious tasks. What we do, we do willingly because we have chosen that particular form of work. We do the work that suits us, for which we have a natural aptitude or talent, the work that brings us the greatest satisfaction, work, moreover, which will produce the best results proportionate to our labour, and which will bring the greatest benefit to others, either directly or indirectly.

No possible service is lost or overlooked or unheeded, or too insignificant to be considered. No matter how small the service may be, it will add to the sum of our spiritual progression without fail. We have no cause to remind anyone of what we have done. Although there is no such mysterious personage as a Recording Angel, yet, somewhere or somehow, our services are converted into the substance of spiritual advancement. We do not pause to ponder how our progression comes about: we are too overjoyed in the reality of it to bother our heads over subjects which it is problematical whether we should understand in the present state of our knowledge.

How many times during the course of your day do you perform some small action for another whose need of help is not actually pressing, but who requires some trivial assistance? You give it, and pass on, and the whole incident has passed from your mind in the space of seconds. You would, in any case, treat it as a commonplace of your natural existence. Reward?—of course not. You do not expect rewards for just directing a fellow passenger to the road for which he is searching. In any case, who is to reward you for such a paltry service? Who, indeed—on earth? Service, my friends, is not confined to either world alone.

Though you may have in mind financial payment for services when I mention the word to you, yet there is much that is performed and passed by where money never enters into the transaction. To put the truth for you in a few words: Service that is performed for a fellow being with no other intention than that of helping him or of bringing him some good is the substance of which spiritual progression is composed. That is not to say that all service done for monetary considerations is itself without other reward.

Bethink you of the numerous occasions during your life on earth when some small addition, in help or advice, say, to that which you have bought and paid for, is freely tendered. All part of the general commercial system, you will say; just good business, that is all. It may be good business, but you reap the benefit. What is most important, the person who extends the kindness reaps the spiritual benefit in service freely given—and both parties will be that much the better. Service need not be counted in money.

Man upon earth hardly realises the interdependence that is the very basis of terrestrial life. It is when a great stoppage occurs in vital services, and people are thrown upon their own resources or must perforce go in want, that the fact of man being dependent upon his fellows is fully comprehended. Man is far more dependent upon his neighbour now than he was hundreds of years ago. Life has since become immensely more complicated and involved. The machinery of earthly existence is so complex and interrelated that when one comparatively small section of it ceases to function, whatever the causes may be, the whole is almost bound to be affected in some measure, great or small.

The economic machinery of the spirit world is always in operation. It never pauses for the fraction of a moment. There is nothing, no possible combination of circumstances, that are ever likely to arise that could lessen or stop the service that is going on continuously. We have our own world to look after, and we have yours as well. With the huge strains that were put upon the spirit world during the recent earthly cataclysm, there was no failure in the services, no break-down. You cannot wage fierce and devastating war upon earth without its effect being transmitted into spirit lands. In many respects our work was far greater than yours. For you were concerned with one world—your own—but we were concerned with two—ours *and* yours. Our work employed vast numbers in its execution.

You will, I have no doubt, recall the old saying about 'counting your blessings'. No advice could be more sound and beneficial. As a corollary to it, I would like to suggest that during the course of one day you count also the various *services* that have been rendered to you. You would be appreciably surprised, I am persuaded.

Whither is all this leading, you may be tempted to enquire? In several directions. I am anxious to show you that in the spirit world work means service, and not just toil. For work has something of a harsh sound, honest though the term may be. After a life of work on earth, to lay stress upon still more work after you have left the earth at your dissolution may fill you with feelings of disappointment, or perhaps of plain revulsion.

We do not toil in these lands. Banish from your minds all ideas of physical fatigue, all monotony, all the hazards of time and circumstances, consequent upon mundane work.

How very precarious can be life upon earth has been evidenced so shockingly of late when the whole earth has been turned upside down, and lives torn asunder, figuratively speaking, by the upheaval. How are you to know that it will not all happen again with even more hideous intensification? Is your life on earth so certain? Indeed, it is not. But of that we will speak again later when I hope to gather together a few threads of thought for your consideration.

The most important point of our discussion is one that is apt to be overlooked. It is this: that man upon earth is not really the dreadful sinner which religion in general would have him to be. There are certain well-established exceptions which it would be needless for me to mention to you. They concern a specific region of the earth, and it is understood that I am now speaking of my friends of earth and *their* friends, and so on.

Man is always understood to have sinned against God pretty well from the beginning, and to have kept up his sinning ever since with varying degrees of intensity. Major wars, plagues, famines, floods and other meteorological disturbances are all 'sent'—so you are taught—by a God who has been so continuously provoked that at last it was imperative that He should retaliate to bring mankind to his senses for the good of his 'immortal soul'. He does so, as it is alleged, by inflicting great punishment upon the people of earth through sufferings of body or mind, or both.

That belief is utterly and completely erroneous. God punishes no man. Man, however, can punish himself, and does so very capably. The Church teaches that man is a 'miserable sinner', and the prayer-books provide documentary evidence in full measure that he is so. Some will believe it; others will not; and more again will not care one way or the other. But the Church never takes into account, because it cannot possibly know, that serving God does not merely consist of assembling people in large numbers at some 'impressive' ceremony of prayer and praise upon one day of the week or another.

Service to God means service to man. How else to serve Him? In elaborate religious ceremonials before large congregations, with the officiating clergy attired in 'full canonicals', and with the choir straining themselves with highly involved music; with eloquent sermons, and long, ornate processions? Or with the utmost simplicity of ritual, in fact, no ritual whatever, but with inordinate psalm and hymn-singing?

Does God demand, or need, or wish for either or both of these extremes? Or being given them, does He accept them as His right, and though not demanding them, yet pleased withal when He receives them? It is a singular misconception of the Father of the Universe, adhered to throughout such wide areas of the earth, that God should require heavy inundations of praise, and such praise, too, that in the end it is naught the most fulsome adulation. Such a misconception is nothing but *pure paganism.*

In ancient days when there was a multiplicity of gods, it was felt that those same gods must be appeased at all costs. It occurred to the simple minds of those times that nothing could be more acceptable to any well-established and self-respecting god than to have a sufficient number of sacrifices and an adequate measure of praise.

Gods needed self-abasement from their votaries—and they got it. They needed ritual of a high degree of mystery and elaboration, and they got it. Those ideas have become firmly and deeply rooted in millions of the earth's inhabitants of whatever religious persuasion so that now you have the utterly untruthful spectacle of the one Universal Father being submitted to the same treatment from organised religion of the present day, and from the same motives and for the same reasons as those of your pagan ancestors. This belief has coloured the whole religious life of the earth world, or rather that part of it known as Christendom.

So many theological errors and fantastic beliefs really have their source in this notion that the Father must be appeased. It vitally alters the whole character of the Father, transforming Him from loving Father into a dreadful Judge and Tyrant, God of Vengeance and Wrath, and making it a high encomium of any man that he should be describe as 'God-fearing'.

The 'fearing', you will be told, in this connection, means reverencing or worshipping and not 'to be afraid of'. Then why not use plain language? There is no merit in fear. It is singular that when one comes to speak of religious matters, words begin to alter their meanings in such ways as would never be tolerated for an instant in other concerns of the earthly life. In religion you may say one thing, while the words you actually employ, being deemed entirely opposite by many people, have a meaning directly opposed to the spoken or written word. Search the termination of the Lord's Prayer, and you will find a glaring example.

No. Serving the Father does not consist in any of the strange performances so widely regarded on earth as true service. Incarnate man can be served in a myriad ways. You do not need me to tell you that! But it is not to say that one can leave out the Father altogether. Very far from it.

You will say that it greatly depends upon whom one serves. The fellow whom you are serving may himself be worthless, and the service may be nothing but a support of base deeds. Of course, that is obvious. The service I am discussing with you has one designation only, and that is the service that is begotten of *loving-kindness*. That one term will at once eliminate all that is not of the highest and purest motives.

The kindness that a man shows to his fellows does not immediately appease a capricious and wrathful God. God is not visibly pleased in such cases, as the pious would have you believe—pleased with you because you have been kind or, on the other hand, wrathful and ready to strike down the person with whom He is not pleased.

Those good actions are reflected upon ourselves; they bring beautiful colours into our spiritual lives, our etheric selves become brighter, and our very raiment adds more and still more lustre to its texture. As you yourselves on earth add one kind action to another, so does your spirit body become brighter, and meet to dwell in the realms of light.

Religious exercises may induce folk to think that they are making some degree of spiritual progression. They may be right or they may be wrong, according to varying circumstances, but there is no doubt whatever about the spiritual results of a kindly action. That, beyond all question, will have done them spiritual good indeed. It is the small services quickly performed, and often unobtrusively and soon forgotten by him who does it, that provide one with such spiritual riches.

How many times have I seen folk awakening here in these beautiful realms of light undergoing the most enjoyable surprise of their lives to find themselves where they are, and not in some dark deep dungeon of hell! Too good to be true, they think, because they 'never professed to be anything,' they will say, when they were on earth. Just so.

But during their lives, of maybe a very humdrum order, they have not forgotten their neighbour. Neither has the law forgotten to act whereby they have registered upon themselves the good that they have done before they came here to dwell.

Such, my dear friends, is the material of which service is made, and by which progression is gained.

Christian Unity

If a religious-minded voyager from another planet were to visit the earth in search of the true religion, what bewilderment would be his; how he would be confounded! It would be remarkable if, at the end of his quest, he departed for his own world with his sanity unimpaired.

Religiously speaking, as well as in many other respects, the earth presents a sad sight to us of the spirit world who are able to see what transpires there. Could that illustrious soul, who spoke to one small comer of the earth nearly two thousand years ago, have ever foreseen or imagined in what manner his words would have been written down, distorted, and later become the material for hundreds upon hundreds of contending religious parties, sects, and denominations?

The word 'sect' is a familiar one to you. It is the habit on earth to address by that title other religious bodies as a means of showing the speaker's own religious superiority, and at the same time expressing contempt and disapproval of another denomination.

Christianity is subdivided into almost numberless individual Churches, with a corresponding profusion of perplexing doctrinal contentions.

When I was upon earth I belonged successively to two denominations—the two principal ones of my native land. Even that statement would be challenged by the parties concerned for neither would acknowledge that the other was the chief. In the second of these two bodies I was ordained priest, and so remained until I passed into the spirit world.

Before I seceded from the first to the second, I went through the usual 'soul-searching', found that I was profoundly dissatisfied with things as they were, and was 'received' into what I fondly believed was the one true Church. That brought me a measure of happiness, or at least contentment of mind. It was not till I arrived here at my dissolution that I saw that I had perturbed myself unnecessarily in the first instance for neither of the two Churches to which I had given my services as a minister was in possession of the truth. That raises a particular point in this subject of the true religion.

Many folk on earth contend that no one religion does or can possess all spiritual truth, but that each religion has some truth in it. It is, however, a statement that leads to very great difficulties. How many religious denominations are there scattered throughout the earth world, that is to say, Christian denominations? There are *hundreds*. How is one to recognise the truth in any whose claims you may choose to examine? Is there any canon by which you could apply a test; any criterion? Those are two questions for you to answer.

You may prefer to weigh the claims and pretensions of one against those of another, and then what? Trust your reason to do the rest? That is what I did when I became dissatisfied with the Church in which I was brought up, and of which my own father was the highest dignitary. I applied reason and logic—at least that is what I supposed myself to be doing. In point of fact, what I did was to examine the claims of both parties side by side, and so I came to the conclusion that the 'party of the second part' spoke with an authority which was completely lacking in the 'party of the first part'.

Then what happened? Proof, such proof as folk *demand* when it is declared that the spirit world exists, and that we, its inhabitants, can visit the earth and speak with our friends there, proof of that kind was wholly absent. I accepted the new position on faith alone, and later assumed the attitude that is common in that religious body—namely, that of spiritual superiority, religious intolerance, and cocksureness. I had 'come home', as my co-religionists are wont to term it.

One used to hear—and you still do so now—much talk about Christian unity. I thought of that in my very early days, and often wondered why the Churches could not unite. When I seceded, I knew the answer—as I thought: mine was the one true Church, and infallible. How could truth be joined to error. All the other religious bodies were in a state of schism or heresy, or both. Even the holy orders which I believed I had possessed were denounced—and still are—as 'absolutely null and utterly void'.

I was, in fact, a layman when I had considered myself a properly ordained minister so that, high dignitary of the Church though my father was, when I seceded and was re-ordained, I was compelled to regard *him* as a layman by force of superior knowledge now that I had the 'true faith'.

Though at first I was a simple priest, yet was I canonically head and shoulders above my father because I had then been ordained *validly*.

How poor, puny, and petty that all seems now. Even when I had made my immediate advent into spirit lands, I felt all this web of theology, which had entangled my mind had I but known it, to be falling away from me in the light of the real, *absolute* truth. I had, upon my secession, relinquished the shadow to grasp the substance (so I thought), but now I found that I had only exchanged one form of shadow for another.

When I met my father here you can imagine how rapturous were our first greetings for we were met at last in the land where the truth abides upon every hand. How amused we were, as we went over together the various conversations we had had on earth, and bethought ourselves of the amount of time and effort and patience we had devoted to discussing the relative claims of at least two Churches. We are now spiritually one in the supreme truth beyond all doubt, disputation, or speculation.

That all or most of the religions on earth have some grain of truth in them, however small, is a statement that itself has a grain of truth in it. If you examine a few of them, you will perceive it for yourself. This is sometimes hailed as a sign of divine wisdom and authenticity, if I may so describe it. The truth, it is averred, cannot be entrusted to one religious body *alone*, but it is split up so that all religions possess a fraction of it which, when combined, make a perfect whole, and it is this combination, or gathering together of the absolute truth, that takes place in heaven. There are no religious controversies in that salubrious place because there one is in the presence of all the religions of earth, and the truth is one at last.

As a theory that is all very well. As a fact it is all very wrong. Certainly you will find some one teaching or another, in any specific religious body, which is a spiritual truth, but what of the rest of the same Church's teachings? For the sake of possessing that one small truth you must also submit to take upon yourself a load of spiritual errors. How are you to select from the whole body of one Church's teaching that which is perfect truth? The only course is not to try—by anything approaching orthodox methods.

As an alternative, and to be sure of being in complete possession of all the truth, you would have to become a member of all the religious denominations of the earth, both great and *small—hundreds and hundreds of them*—so as to be certain of not missing one fragment of the truth. That would be manifestly impossible, earthly life being so short. Even then, the problem would not be solved for you would still be uncertain—to put it mildly—what was true spiritual teaching and what was not.

Would it not be possible, do you think, to write down in parallel columns upon a very large sheet of paper the multiform teachings of all the Churches, observing closely where the teachings or beliefs were exactly similar, or close enough for working purposes, then noting what was common to all and most repeated in some, and so strike a balance or effect a compromise? That way, I fear, would your difficulties only increase.

Such method is something of the kind that is in the churchmen's minds when the cry for Christian unity goes up. Would it not be possible, they plead, for some least common factor to be found upon which all Christian Churches could agree, and upon this basis unite, just as in the early days the Church was one and undivided? *Was it?* Was the Church ever in that perfect state?

History and historians seem to declare that the Church was always troubled with heresy, and by its members becoming dissatisfied with things as they were, and going off and founding religions of their own. Schisms and heresies have always existed. But could not *one* Church or religious body (still to persist in the matter) be distinguished from all others as being the first, the absolute first, devolving without question from its founder?

At last we seem to have arrived at our destination through our 'progress backwards' in history and time. Of course, there must be an absolute first, but which, it is most difficult to say for there are several claimants, each strenuously and with loud voice denying the others.

When I was on earth I thought I had found the first and original, the only Church. Everything seemed to point that way. It was comparatively easy to dispose of the claims of the others by listening to the voice of Authority. The Church to which I had previously belonged always boasted that it did not lay down any rigid canons of belief, but allowed its people to exercise their own private judgement, and think and believe practically what they liked. In this way, all schools of religious thought could be included within the one framework of the establishment.

This, in effect, was what had always been done in this particular Church ever since its foundation— liberty of thought, private judgement—until the liberty became a little too free and unrestrained, when the fires were lighted and the heretics burned for their rashness and wickedness. They were martyrs for the faith. Their crown of martyrdom has since become slightly tarnished in the eyes of many of the incarnate.

It is not an edifying spectacle to witness all this ecclesiastical wrangling, with claim and counterclaim, as well as accusation and acrimony within the structure of a 'divinely instituted Church'.

How would our visitant from another planet view all this? With what feelings? He would note many things, just as we observe them from the spirit world. We see, for one thing, dwindling congregations in the Churches. Some of the clergy have also noticed it themselves, and those in authority say that the world is rapidly turning heathen and godless.

Decay has set in in the Churches, and no one can stop it. They wonder why. They ask a few people for their opinion, who say that they do not go to Church anymore because the services are, for one thing, so dull. Such a reply sorrowfully surprises the ministers because religious worship should not be spoken of in terms of dullness. Church services are not a form of amusement or light recreation. They are beautiful, and the language of the liturgy itself is inspiring—especially those portions of it which the congregation cannot understand.

The Church accuses the laity of degenerating into pagans because, by their congregational absence, they have abandoned God, and now worship materialism. They find (it is alleged) the worldly counter-attractions too compelling to be withstood upon the one day of the week when they should turn their minds to God in worship in His Church. Abolish the counter-attractions of the Sunday, say some, and that would help to fill the Churches.

Would it really—and with *willing* worshippers? This smacks uncommonly of compulsion. Does God require or demand compulsion in His worship? Does not this suggest paganism at its worst—the very paganism of which the Church condemns the laity? The services as they stand at present—and they have not altered appreciably since my days on earth—literally reek of paganism.

Approach the prayerbook with an absolutely free mind, clear of all preconceptions upon the nature and character of the Father of Heaven and Earth, and examine the prayers for yourself. What do you see? As though you were an analytical expert seeing them for the first time, what can you deduce from the set form of prayers? You would be compelled to say that whoever

God may be to whom you are addressing your ejaculations and petitions, this is His character as revealed by the writers of the prayers.

By the very framing of the sentences, their preambles, their contents, and their terminations, the writers must be supposed to know and understand something of the nature of the Being to whom the prayers are being directed. Your analysis might read thus: The God whom you worship must be gratified with much homage since so much stress is laid upon the word worship.

It is impossible to deduce what pleasure or profit He can derive from such *exaggerated* adulation. It is manifestly wrong by all canons of spiritual conduct to accord worship to any human individual or thing upon earth as to a god. What effect, if any, can there be upon the one supreme Being of great surges of praise arising to Him from the people of earth, *assuming that such praise ever reaches Him?*

It must be concluded that this praise is earnestly believed to be acceptable to the Deity, and must make Him favourably inclined towards whatever requests and petitions are to accompany it. It would appear that all supplications must be prefaced by extreme adulation before any reasonable hope can be entertained that the prayerful request will be granted.

In the event of the prayer not being answered, and no reason being able to be assigned for its failure, it must, by the use of such phrases as 'Thy will be done,' be assumed that the answer to prayer depends not so much upon its merits or urgency, but upon the particular whim of God. Wherefore it may be presumed that He is of uncertain temperament—that is, capricious. That He is of pronounced uncertain temper is evidenced by the varied headings under which the prayers are comprised, where, for instance, protection is sought from storms and other meteorological disturbances of varying nature, from famines. For a truly benevolent God would never visit His children with such calamities as are generally believed to have their source in the Deity.

The occurrence of war, for example, is usually attributed to the wrath of God being visited upon a sinful or erring nation or world. The wrath of God is mentioned in some of the prayers, and though wrath itself on occasion may be righteous, so it is claimed, yet it is never a pleasant emotion to be openly displayed, especially when it is the direct cause of wars in which so many thousands of the innocent are bound to suffer. True justice would therefore not seem to be part of the Deity's character for in no sense can that be strict justice where the innocent are punished with the guilty. Nor is there evidence of strict justice where so much mercy is pleaded, and so often, and presumably with the hope of receiving it. For where does true justice enter in where mercy is extended?

Is not the intelligence of the supreme Being grossly underrated when certain irrelevant interpolations are made in the prescribed order of the services? The Ten Commandments, for instance, are said to have emanated from God. Can it afford Him any pleasure, therefore, to hear them recited in numerical order as part of the liturgy in His worship? Were it merely necessary to remind the congregations of the existence of the Ten Commandments, could they not be so recalled without obtruding upon the service of worship itself? It must be assumed then that their recital carries with it some talismanic value, which in itself seems a reversion to the primitive times when superstition was only a trifle more widespread than it is today.

The conclusions to be drawn from the openings of all prayers is that God must be placated and appeased by fulsome adulation, for which He has an obvious weakness, and that they must be terminated by references to theological doctrine whose obscurity of meaning must leave those who utter the prayers in extreme doubt as to the purport of what they are saying. It would appear that meaningless though the words may be, no prayer, for some inexplicable reason, can be considered of any value whatsoever without their recital.

The claim that God is all love is greatly confused and largely contradicted by the numerous begging appeals against the visitation of all manner of calamities, of which, it is to be supposed, He is the source, and for which no rationally minded person on earth has ever been able to perceive the just cause.

Those are some of the conclusions which you might reasonably be expected to draw were you to read a prayerbook for the first time, and with a mind perfectly clear of any bias, prejudices, or preconceptions, religious or otherwise.

Orthodox religion is founded upon a series of dreadful errors, the most outrageous of which is the monstrous idea of the nature of the Father of the Universe.

The cry is for Christian unity. Suppose it were to be brought about, what then? Would it solve all problems, or any problems at all? There was a time when the Church was very nearly one. Were those days any better than the present times? Can the Church prevent the most horrific of all occurrences—the occurrence of war—which has gone on intermittently through the passage of the centuries, yet so persistently as to introduce into at least one language the terms 'war-time' and 'peace-time'.

Does not the Church, by implication and by its actions, approve of war? If not, how does it come about that its ministers should bless with ceremonial the very implements of war? Is it not to make a mockery of God to ask His benediction upon instruments that are to be employed in the killing of men?

Why has the Church been riven with divisions and controversies and rivalries of sufficient ferocity to make men hate their neighbours, to cause acts to be passed for the suppression of religious liberty whereby the offender shall be burnt at the stake for his 'heresy' or his 'apostasy' or his 'schism', or tortured in the name of Holy Religion?

Why has the Church failed, and failed dismally? These are many questions, my friends, for you to answer, if you wish, according to your views.

What is the truth as we know it in the spirit world? The spirit world, it would be surmised, is the one place where all religious problems must be resolved. A correct surmise. Then how could Christian unity be achieved? There is only one way.

It might be thought that if one could possibly get all people to think alike upon the subject of religion, then unity would be quickly and easily brought about. But people thought almost alike in the days when the Church was presumed to be one and undivided. Nevertheless the divisions came, because people began to think *not* alike. In other words, they began to think differently, and it must be allowed that all men, of whatever nation or period of time, should be at liberty to think differently from their neighbours.

Of course. No one could quarrel with that. In the spirit world we can *think* what we like, but our thoughts, as with you, are regulated or influenced by our knowledge. Religious unity can never come about upon a basis of what men *think*, though they may, at least for the time, think alike. It must be based upon what they *know*. It must be based upon as full a knowledge of the facts as it is possible to acquire.

Religious unity founded upon spiritual truth, absolute truth, is the only unity that can endure. There is no disputing that which is truth, *absolute* truth, ascertained and proved to be such. Religious truth as dispensed by Orthodoxy is more often than not merely the expressed opinions of doctors and fathers of the Church.

Unity based upon opinions cannot last. Unity based upon natural spiritual laws will abide forever. Is not the science of mathematics founded upon fact, numerical truth? Who is there who would dispute the multiplication tables? Has there been any schism among mathematicians because some scientist expressed his opinion that two and two are five? Is it ever likely to happen? Never, so long as sanity prevails throughout the earth.

Religion, as it is generally understood, concerns among other things the welfare of the spiritual part of man, and it is the most vitally important of all subjects under the earthly sun. But religion is a veritable battleground of contention where it should rest upon a high degree of exactitude acquired from absolute knowledge. If the religions had less of opinion and more of knowledge, disruption would begin to vanish with the rapidity of morning mist in the warmth of the rising sun.

If the Churches do really and sincerely desire to become one, their only hope of ever achieving unity is by discovering the spiritual truth, and in the light of it casting out from their creeds and doctrines every article that is against that truth. There will then be no need to place their doctrinal cards upon the table for all to see. There will be no need to search for a least common factor upon which all can find some measure of agreement. Verity speaks for itself. Its voice is clear and clamant, and cannot be gainsaid.

What are the possibilities of such unity ever being brought about under the conditions that I have suggested to you? As we view matters in the spirit world, there will surely come a time when the truth will be diffused throughout the earth. That is bound to happen eventually. Perhaps you will say that since the Church was first instituted, hundreds of years ago, affairs have become steadily worse, the divisions have increased in number and range, while many strange religious sects have arisen in all parts of the earth, each holding the most bizarre beliefs. Of the latter, one need scarcely take heed. They are mostly the outcome of slightly disordered minds, and they will disappear in time.

The Church that first came into being is not comparable with the numerous organisations known collectively under that appellation today. Was a Church *instituted*? The great founder of Christianity, so-called, was not the least interested in founding any Church. In good truth, *he* founded no Church in spite of the alleged references to 'my' Church. He had no intention of establishing Church or Chapel nor any other form of religious organisation. He came to give simple teaching to simple folk, showing them how to live their lives on earth, and how to behave towards their neighbours.

He told them that the God of wrath, as they understood Him to be, was indeed no God of wrath at all, but the Father of all love. He told his hearers that death of the physical body was not the end of all things, but the real beginning of life, a new life in the immense world of the spirit. He told them that such gifts as he possessed and demonstrated, of healing the sick and speaking spiritual truths, were not mystical or magical gifts, nor were they operated through the power of the devil, but that they were natural gifts which they could themselves develop and use in the service of their fellows, it they went about it in the right way.

He showed his hearers how the mourner could and should be comforted in the only possible way, for the so-called dead were not dead; they were very much alive, and could speak in precise, clear terms, just as he was then addressing his audience. That it was right and proper to do so was evidenced, among other things, by the great consolation which such communication brought to the bereaved in being able to speak once again with those whom they had thought had passed for ever from their ken. That was what the founder of Christianity told his followers. How does that compare with the extraordinary and unnatural beliefs of the first and undivided Church? Strangely, indeed.

As the present Church claims to be the lineal descendant of that early Church, it is simple enough to see the wide disparity between the teaching of Jesus and the queer collection of doctrines and dogmas now held by the Church. If the theorists wish to refer to the primitive Church, they must eventually go still farther back, and it will mean a wholesale reconstruction of their beliefs, with the equally wholesale elimination of the many religious practices which have no approximation to the truth nor any value whatever spiritually.

The Church must in fact start *de novo*, sweeping the board clear of all the theological rubbish and accumulation which have been piled upon it during the passing of the centuries. If they were to study the life of the Master Christian even from the scanty chronicles that exist, and *copy his methods*, they would have something solid upon which to build their Christian unity. The theological forest has become obscured by its own distorted and too abundant trees.

There was a time in history when men developed a passion for reforming the Church. At least, that is what they called it. The reforms which they introduced were mostly the outcome of muddled thinking, with very occasionally a minute move in the right direction. But in casting out some belief which was considered no longer tenable, they substituted others equally without truth, and generally caused so much hatred, not only of themselves but of their new ideas, that feelings ran high, and blood flowed, while the list of the 'martyrs' grew. Of what use such reforms as those?

The Church of the present time has grown highly organised. It is much concerned with affairs of the earth as they affect it ecclesiastically, but the great world of the spirit is woefully neglected. The one institution on earth which, by virtue of its very claims and functions, should be most actively in communion with all, is cut off and separated from us. *The whole Christian Church is in a state of 'schism' with us of the spirit world!*

To the great bulk of the clergy, the spirit world is a silent world of the dead. They cannot answer the straightforward questions of a despairing soul: what has become of my dear ones who have left this earth? Where are they? Why is there this cruel silence, and why cannot you, the appointed (*self-appointed*) ministers of God's Church, give us, who are so deeply in sorrow, some real comfort, some truth?

We do not want speculations; we do not wish now to hear about God's mercy—that will not dry our tears, nor stop their flow. We do not wish to hear quotations from the scriptures about faith, nor to be given spurious comfort from a book hundreds of years old. Our loved ones passed from this earthly life this very week. Why turn to a book so old when we are speaking of now, this actual moment of time, *within the week of our sad loss?*

You say to us *blessed are they that mourn, for they shall be comforted.* If you insist upon throwing that text at us, then where is that comfort? Give us the comfort, not some religious counterfeit.

How would you, my dear friends, have answered such a despairing cry from the heart had you been in my position when I was on earth? Yet as a minister of the Church I should have been able to answer such an afflicted soul with the truth. Alas, I could not; all that I could do was call for the exercise of faith upon the part of the distressed one, and to have hope and trust in God's mercy, backed by the powerful intercession of the true Church.

For had not the departed soul been 'fortified by the rites of our Holy Mother the Church'? Incidentally, so had I when my time came to depart, but I cannot say that those rites availed me anything whatever!

What word of real consolation had I to offer when some sad soul came to me for help? I could not give of my knowledge, for of knowledge I had none. Whatever I might have guessed or thought privately, it was not my business to reveal what was in my mind concerning the 'afterlife', but to speak upon the Church's teaching and authority alone, and the Church had 'no statement to make.'

However secure I felt in other circumstances with the might of the Church behind me. in such moments as these we are discussing I realised to the full my helplessness through ignorance. I could talk freely and fluently upon the sacraments, upon the Church's teaching concerning this or that. I could urge more faith upon the part of my suppliant: I could offer my own prayers, which I can see now served precious little purpose because they were altogether upon the wrong lines.

I could advise others to pray, too, and leave it for them to find the words of their supplication. My rejoicing at being a member of the One True Church was, at such times as these, somewhat tempered—to put it mildly—when in cases of real spiritual need, the best I had to offer was empty hollow phrases upon stereotyped lines, and trust to time to dim the memory and heal the sore of affliction of those who came to see me.

The founder of Christianity had more to tell his listeners about the welfare of the soul after the death of the physical body than have all the Churches of Christendom this very day.

Christian unity as envisaged by the clergy and laity is a state where the whole earth is conforming, more or less, to the one body of teaching, where the members of one persuasion are in communion with those of another. And would the earth be any the better for such unity? None whatever, for it would merely be a unity of error.

Though the unity might endure for a measurable time, yet in the end it would be bound to be dissevered once again, and so repeat the whole performance of divisions and schisms and controversies. The Church on earth at these present times is worn out because it has *nothing* to offer any thinking man or woman but lifeless doctrines. Indeed, the Church itself is lifeless despite the appearance of activity that is to be observed.

How shall the Church be regarded? By results? What are they? The Church is powerless to prevent wars upon earth because it has no influence with the governments of the earth. Were the Churches to unite upon a common platform of 'No War,' who in authority would listen? The religious teachers accept war as a punishment of God for the world's wickedness. And if such were the case, then it must be manifestly wrong to cry out against or condemn what has been declared as a just and divine punishment. Such are the tortuous, serpentine ways of the theologians!

Christian unity is far more concerned with ancient ecclesiastical history, with valid or invalid orders, with ceremonial and ritual and vestments, with rubric, with Church buildings and appurtenances, and with preferment and livings. The leaders of religion are occasionally to be observed rapping the laity upon the knuckles ever so gently because they do not attend the services in sufficiently large numbers, and because they profane the Sabbath with material enjoyments instead of packing the Church and giving evidence of how virile religion really is.

Viewed from the inside, there is religious intolerance and self-satisfaction; viewed from the outside—from the spirit world—we can see just how much a mockery of the truth is Orthodoxy. Hundreds of years of false teachings that have had to be set right with the unhappy victims of them in the spirit world. The institution that is supposed to send its members fully equipped for the journey into the 'great beyond', in fact sends its voyagers all-ignorant of spiritual knowledge, ill-equipped in every way, and so often paralysed with fear of what is to happen to them.

If you wish to know whether the Churches have failed, ask us of the spirit world, and we can provide you with a plain unequivocal answer in one short word: Yes. If all the Churches of the earth were to unite in their present state of ignorance, the failure would still continue.

It is customary for ministers to cast their, minds back wistfully into the past, to those days of religious unity which they call 'the age of Faith'. Let them turn their minds in another direction, to the age of Fact, of fact acquired, secured, and proved, and casting all their theological speculations aside, base a real Unity upon spiritual truth, for mighty is the truth, and it will prevail.

Peace on Earth

We had made a brief pause in our labours, and we were enjoying what in our earthly days we should have called a 'day-off'. By 'we' I mean a small company consisting of some artists and musicians, all of them masters of their craft; my former religious superior, who was a prince of the Church; my father, who was also a noted prelate of his times, but of a denomination opposed to mine; and lastly, my good friends and present colleagues, Edwin and Ruth. We formed a most pleasant company of companions.

It would have done the hearts of advocates for religious unity on earth the greatest good to have observed my father and my former superior themselves in complete unity! They have become fast friends in these lands, and frequently meet beneath my roof. Indeed, my father has upon many occasions expressed his gratitude to my quondam superior for his care of me during the latter part of my earthly life, when he, as it were, stood in *loco parentis*.

On the occasion of which I am now speaking, we had all of us temporarily abandoned our work, not—I would hasten to add—from any causes of disaffection, but by a prearranged plan we had so disposed our various activities and made the necessary provision where we were closely engaged, that we could in company recreate ourselves according to our particular whims and desires. And so we disported ourselves in all manner of ways, called in a body upon other friends, and generally passed hither and thither with no special object in view but that of enjoyment in recreation.

The musicians and painters, though music and art is their principal work, also direct their labours into other channels. Consequently, they are full of business and bustling affairs, as we all are.

Now we were seated in comfortable chairs beneath the trees upon the lawn of my house, breathing the sweet-scented air, with the beautiful gardens round about us, free of every care, chatting merrily upon a wide variety of subjects, and exchanging experiences of every kind. Their range was extensive, as you can well imagine, among such a mixed company whose earthly and spirit-world activities were so diversified.

Of the whole of our gathering perhaps the worst off were the musicians for they were called upon to provide music for our entertainment. The painters, however, by virtue of their profession, claimed instant exemption from any active performance, and they at once became extremely self-satisfied upon the strength of it! As one of them remarked, he would be delighted to paint a picture for us there and then, but as it would take some time to do, since a picture cannot be painted in a moment, it would be as well to make ample provision for someone to carry on our work for us, while we made ourselves as comfortable as possible in preparation for an extremely long session for he was an extremely slow workman, and tended to become even slower when working in the presence of others!

For our further entertainment we were offered a course of sermons by our clerical friends upon a number of subjects, all of which we resolutely declined without thanks. It seemed therefore that our musicians were the most handicapped of us all, but they enjoyed themselves heartily none the less.

We were seated thus when Ruth's quick eye perceived two men in the distance evidently coming in our direction. As they proceeded, they paused here and there to look at the flowers, until at length they were sufficiently near for us to identify them. One was a man of commanding presence whose most marked feature was his raven-black hair.

I first introduced him and his constant companion to you in the very earliest of these writings as the Chaldean and the Egyptian. Since my early days in spirit lands, they have both been my kindest friends, always ready to help and advise upon every occasion and to give me the benefit of their experience gained through a long, a very long, life in the spirit world. At once I went forward to greet our two visitors, who were equally well known to the whole of our present company.

We were naturally delighted beyond words that they should have chosen such a moment for their visit. My friends rose in a body upon the approach of our visitants, and there was a free exchange of the most cordial greetings. In the meantime, Ruth and one of the men had disappeared indoors, reappearing shortly after with a special chair which we reserved for such guests. It was a very substantial oaken armchair, heavily carved, and was altogether a great favourite. With many warm expressions the Chaldean seated himself in it, with Ruth at his right hand and the Egyptian at his left.

The Chaldean had come, he said, upon business as well as pleasure. At the mention of the word business, our friends made a movement of withdrawing, thinking that he would wish to discuss whatever matter it may be, without other auditors. But the Chaldean would not hear of it and bade them all be re-seated.

He understood, he said, that a vast deal of talking had been going on during our assembly, and therefore he felt that a little more would do no harm whatever. The Chaldean, I should add, is a man whose sense of humour is keen, and that to be in his presence is always a mental tonic. He is a living testimony to the fact that those who dwell in the highest realms do not lose their light-heartedness and humour.

It was a pity, he said, that we had refused the excellent offer from our colleagues of listening to a sermon or two as he could see, he added, that the whole company would be none the worse for a little extra spiritual tone!

After a further exchange of pleasantries, the Chaldean turned to me and spoke of our prospective writings, of which these present are the accomplishment. He then made the suggestion that perhaps I would favour the insertion of a chapter upon a theme which he had to offer. I expressed my willingness and delight to be of every possible service to him. He voiced his pleasure and proceeded to outline to me the subject he wished discussed. I was to use my own words, he merely supplying a conspectus.

We listened with interest while he set forth the various points of his narration. Some of our company, who were not so conversant with earthly matters as others of us, were saddened by what the Chaldean had to recount. At length the matter was disposed of, and the conversation became our own once more. Our party resumed its lighter temper after the gravity of our visitor's discourse, and being pressed to remain as long as possible, our two visitors joined with us in our mild conviviality, to which the Chaldean's jocundity and wealth of experiences added greatly. Thus we continued.

So, before our present company disbands, as it were, each upon his own particular occasions and without further preamble, here is what I was bid to discuss with you.

Upon every day, of every week, of every year on earth, the ejaculation goes forth that was reputed to have been made so long, long ago by an angelic host in a little corner of the earth: *Glory to God in the highest, and on earth peace to men of good will.*

For how many hundreds of years has that sentence been uttered? And upon how many occasion has the earth's peace been shattered? The pages of history books are stained with the blood of human beings shed in the countless wars that have assailed the earth, each of them growing more intense, each of them producing an ever increasing number of victims. With the multiplication of scientific discoveries upon every hand, it seems to have been inevitable that wherever possible those discoveries should be turned to mortal account upon the advent of war. The weapons of war have, in some measure, ceased to be used individually, and have been turned into instruments of wholesale slaughter whose sufferers are counted in thousands of thousands.

These are matters upon which you, my good friends, are only too well informed through your own bitter experiences of a recent past, and I thus lay them before you, not to waste your time nor try your patience by telling you of something of which you are fully aware, but because a plain statement of the obvious is sometimes advisable in order to make a chosen theme perfectly clear.

Life upon earth has become hazardous. My friends have doubtless asked themselves why it is that, seemingly, war has always existed on earth, and, further, why cannot wars be ended for all time? You would be answered by your neighbour that that is precisely what the leaders of the whole world are now so sedulously trying to do.

Now here I want to make a declaration that is as plain and unequivocal, as unyielding and spiritually indisputable, as the words of language can make it. It is a spiritual truth, the profundity of which few leaders on earth have ever bothered to consider with any degree of real seriousness, but which is nevertheless to be found within the prayer-books and incorporated in the services of at least one State Church. This is it: *Thou shalt not kill.* Look in your prayer-books, and you will find that it is placed fifth, *fifth*, on the list of God's commandments!

What is the spiritual law governing human earthly life in this respect? In other words, what does the spirit world say? It says just what I have said to you, but in any list of spiritual prohibitions it allots a far higher place than *fifth*.

By what right does man on earth assume to himself the power over 'life and death', as it is termed? It is the custom on earth to legitimatize the killing of human beings by the passing of enactments. (You have witnessed at least one country which dispensed with such legalities in favour of verbal instructions, or the briefest of hand-written documents). So that by incorporating into the laws of a country official permission to kill human beings, that act is made right and proper, is not that so? It matters not whether the case concerns the individual or whether it concerns a whole nation as a militant force. It is the nature of governments—and of many state-aided Churches as well—to regard the people over whom they have assumed authority to consider those people only in relation to the earth world.

The earth is essentially—to them—the real world, the material world. It is *life,* the only life that is known, but scarcely understood. Death of the physical body is, of course, inevitable, they will concede, but with that they are not concerned. It is the Church's duty to look after that in the way it deems best, and subject to whatever control and influence the state may exercise in its direction and the appointment of its ministers and dignitaries.

There may be a nominal combination of Church and State, but the latter has little or no interest in the former. The Church is all very well for the pious and other religious minded folk, and the members of a governing body may say some formal prayer before any official proceedings are opened. It is done as a matter of custom, and little if any significance is placed upon the action. They may pray for guidance in their deliberations, but in the end, they prefer to rely upon their own sage judgement.

By every spiritual law, as we are familiar with them in the spirit world, it is wrong to legalise in any form the power of terminating the natural period of any person's life upon earth. To employ the terms of part of an enactment that was responsible for ecclesiastical dis-unity in my own native land, 'no prince, person, prelate, state or potential spiritual or temporal' has the right 'to exercise a manner of power, jurisdiction, superiority, authority. pre-eminence or privilege' over spiritual law of which *thou shalt not kill* occupies a *prominent position.*

What does the law of earth say in this connection as applied to the individual and to whole nations? In the case of the individual, it says in effect: This person has committed a breach of the law by killing another person. We therefore have no further use for him in this world. We know nothing whatever about the laws of the next world, but the next world must take him and have him. He is too bad for our world. We have judged him, and found him guilty. God will now do the same, albeit we commend his soul to God's mercy. Ostensibly we do this as a deterrent to others, but in truth we wish to be rid of him, because that is the cheapest and most satisfactory way of dealing with him.

In the case of nations, it is the custom to settle international disagreements and arguments, where words and negotiation have failed, by a recourse to arms. The nations meet one another as circumstances dictate, and the armed forces of the nations, that is to say, its citizens, who are human beings, will proceed to kill each other by such means as may be suitable or available or according to the exigencies of the place and time.

This method of dealing with international disputes, failing all pacific means, is a custom established through such a long period of years as to have no date assignable for its actual incipience. The armed forces have the power given them to kill the enemies of the state. You see, my friends, I am setting down literally the method used by the rulers of your earth to settle the earth's quarrels. It is: go to war, and *kill, kill, kill*. Hunt the enemy and kill him.

Before I go a step further you will exclaim to me: 'That's all very well, but what was to be done? You have seen for yourselves, at least, we presume you have done so—to what extremes we were forced at the outset of the recent hostilities. We have tried to preserve the world from becoming one vast slave state, and its inhabitants from every kind of bestiality. We represented *right* as opposed to *might*. We had to defend our very lives and homes, and try to keep safe a decent world for ourselves and our children.'

That is your situation as you would describe it to me. Then let me say to you that with it we, of the spirit world, have the fullest sympathy. That you were battling with the worst evil that has yet assailed the earth there is no disputing whatever, and any man who would do otherwise is just plainly a fool.

Do not forget, my friends, that we saw more of this evil than ever did you, though you yourselves may have been in the very thick of the fighting. We were able to perceive what forces, unseen by you, and in most cases never dreamt of by you, were at work striving upon the side of wrong. But let me say again that it is still wrong—and ever will be—for man to kill fellow-man, for any reason whatsoever. Whatever the reasons, whatever the provocations, it is yet wrong. We must not go against the law of God, which is the spiritual law.

There is an old saying, with which you are very familiar, that two blacks do not make a white. That is an everlasting truth, and no new discovery, or other and further spiritual revelation, can alter it or dispose of it, or in any way upset it. But in the case of war, it has become the order that the end justifies the means— a dangerous doctrine.

How do wars come about? The history books will inform you upon the political situations that finally led to the outbreak of each war. It is not happy reading, and fully reveals the spiritual blindness of the earth world. Some folk say that if only the teachings of the great soul who is named the Prince of Peace were put into practice *absolutely and without default*, then wars would end for all time on earth.

How is that to be done? Through the influence of the Churches? That would seem to be the obvious way. But what of the misdeeds that have been, and are, done in God's name or in that of Holy Religion? History also tells of those. Have heretics never been burnt at the stake? True, it was the secular arm that actually did the burning, *not*, of course, the Church. The latter only condemned. That is what the Church would have you to believe. The Church could, however, have cried aloud against such barbarities, but did not, because it thought nothing could be too awful in the way of punishment for a heretic.

The Church once had powerful jurisdiction. It can do nothing now but utter moral condemnation, which it seldom does. When it does, it is never heeded. The Church must bow to the State—which is, perhaps, just as well when burnings at the stake are called to mind.

In turning to the Scriptures for a code of moral behaviour, you must carry in your mind the diversified interpretations of those Scriptures which have resulted in Christian disunity. You will perhaps say that the commandment *Love one another,* needs no interpretation, and you would be undeniably right. This subject of scriptural interpretation has already been discussed with you elsewhere.

All that I will say now upon this point is that the Scriptures do not contain all that the great teacher spoke, and that the great bulk of his teachings are not contained within the covers of the book which is universally used on earth at this day. Had the full text been retained and omissions supplied, perhaps a very different story might have been told of the earth's subsequent spiritual journey through the ages.

War under any designation must for ever remain spiritually condemned, whether it be punitive, aggressive, or for other causes that need no enumerating. In many directions is the earth spiritually blind, but in none so hopelessly as in resorting to arms as a means of settling disputes. Here you see the results of the Church's teaching, or the lack of it.

If the Church had possessed any spiritual truths at all, this gross undervaluation of human life on earth would never have taken root and endured for centuries, as it has done. The laws concerning human life on earth are based upon crude theology and error. The laws of a nation must be respected in the sense that they must be obeyed, but no nation has the power, divinely speaking, or the right of mandate to shorten by one second of time the natural tenure of man's life on earth. The council of the nations think otherwise, but in that they are disastrously wrong.

Let me now turn to another aspect of this subject You must know that no person of whatsoever social position or spiritual status is ever left unattended by us at the moment of his dissolution whether that passing is taking place on the land, or in the air, upon the waters, or beneath them.

Whether we can approach that individual rests upon his own spiritual state or condition. If we are able to approach and offer our assistance, we do so without fail. Our advances may be scorned or spurned; the passing soul may be so steeped in evil as to make approach impossible. Nevertheless, someone will be at hand to do whatever is humanly possible. If we see that we can do nothing, we reluctantly withdraw.

In normal times on earth our work goes steadily on as the passage of folk to these land takes its regular course with its customary numbers. With the advent of modern warfare, these numbers are prodigiously increased and their rate of entry into these lands vastly accelerated. To so many still left on earth, these souls, civilians or soldiers, have 'gone hence', and that is all that can be said for what has overtaken them or how they fare, no man knows, no man can guess. That is the general attitude of those who have no real spiritual knowledge.

Early in these present writings I have spoken to you of the changes that have occurred in these and other realms consequent upon two wars, and I have also touched upon the enormous amount of extra work which has to be undertaken when such wars break out on earth. We have seen the last frightful conflict from a side that was impossible to you yet incarnate.

We, in these lands, have seen, among other things, all the loathsome hatred that has been inspired by the thwarting of evil men's base designs, hatred, moreover, that has been carried into the spirit world hard and fast upon the miscreants who were harbouring it in their dark souls. Of those I will speak in a moment.

I have reminded you that our works of service were so increased that the word 'colossal' becomes almost insignificant with which to define their magnitude. How many persons, would you say, have passed into these lands whose passing was caused by this last war? Their number has been moderately computed by your earthly chroniclers as *thirty millions*. That is an understatement.

For many it was a release from inexpressible horrors and barbarities and tortures, committed upon them by the followers of the most evil of all men of modern times. His followers themselves were no less evil, but the chief inspirer of the abominations was himself inspired from the darkest realms of the spirit world.

By whom are these dark realms inhabited? They are inhabited by people who formerly lived upon earth. It is not the spirit world that has made them what they are, nor placed them where they are—in the uttermost darkness. It is their life on earth that has fitted them for it. Some of them have been sent there prematurely by the laws of the earth-plane; others have gone there eventually at their normal passing; and the wars have helped to increase their numbers. Therefore would I ask you to remember that it is the earth life that has caused the spiritual descent of these souls, not the subsequent life in the spirit world.

The last great war was brought about by an overflowing of these sunken souls on to the earth plane where, all unseen by you, they found that by a combined effort they could easily inspire an evil-minded man and his evil-minded supporters and cohorts.

That hideous war was not sent by God as a punishment for the earth's sins. That is a stupid fiction invented by stupid churchmen whose 'understanding' of the Father of love is begotten of their crude, pagan theology. To believe and affirm that God inflicted such torturing punishment upon incarnate mankind is a defamation of the grossest description, for it drags Him down to the level of some pagan tribal god.

The incarnate instruments of evil took the path of ruin, and proceeded headlong down it. It might be asked: if these people on earth were inspired by the denizens of the dark realms of the spirit world, how is it that they were so successful, up to a point? Why was not their initial success followed by a complete and final victory for evil?

The answer is that these infamous creatures of the dark realms are interested in their incarnate instruments only to the extent of fulfilling their desires, and it is part of their scheme that their instruments shall be brought to ultimate downfall. It is not their aim to provide victories for anyone, but only in as much as it serves their present purpose. Their last purpose is to bring ruin upon all who have any dealings with them, to drag down others to their own low and obscene level.

They themselves have seemingly sunk so low that it is impossible for them to sink any deeper. They have nothing to lose, but much to gain in the devilish delight which the sight of human downfall can afford them. Terrestrial conditions were such that this enormous eruption of evil from the dark regions was made possible. Step by step, the wicked plan was built up, with what results it is needless for me to remind you.

After great travail the evil forces were banished, and now, what remains? Are you at peace? Many of you—indeed, most of you—will say you are very far from it for upon every hand and in almost every part of the earth there unrest and economic turmoil. Naturally, you will expect some time to elapse before a full return can be made to those conditions of life which you all envisage belonging to 'peace-time'.

So many years of energy being devoted entirely to war pursuits have denuded the earth of so much that is now sorely needed, alike for bare necessities as for ordinary comfort. But that apart, there is at this moment too much unrest. That is not surprising. The nations of the earth are exhausted from a military point of view, even as they are exhausted in their physical bodies from the years of toil and strain and bad nourishment. Nerves that are frayed make tempers short. But there are other reasons for this unrest. We will come to them in a moment.

I would ask you to bethink yourself of what I have mentioned to you regarding the *fifth* commandment. You have witnessed a group of evil men being brought to the bar of earthly justice to answer for their monstrous crimes against the whole earth. That they should have been so brought is meet and just. Writers upon the subject have given it as their opinion that only time will prove whether this was a good thing to do or a bad thing.

As we see matters in the spirit world, the company of nations have done right in causing these inhuman beings to be brought before them, and condemning them before the whole world. The verdict of guilty was a proper one. None other could have been brought with *true justice*—of which the earth knows so little. But with the condemnation of a number of them to be despatched forthwith into these lands of the spirit, the people of these realms and of every realm of light above us and below, are in absolute and total disagreement.

What has been done beyond any question or doubt? The earth is rid of these men, and you feel that you can now breathe more freely. You feel that the root of the trouble has been dug up, and systematically and finally destroyed. The arch-perpetrators are no longer on earth, and therefore they can cause no more trouble. Can they not? Can *they not indeed?*

What has actually been done, then? *This:* instead of keeping all these monsters of iniquity, or as many of them as did not take their departure for the dark realms by their own hand, where you would know them to be, where you could always find them, and where they could do no more harm; instead of keeping them in close confinement, the leaders of the earth *have set them free.* They are now here in these lands of the spirit world, *free.*

Free to exert their wicked wills upon any whom they can find. Free to unite, as they were united on earth; free to return to the earth unseen by you, there to stir up every manner of trouble where they can discover any who will listen to their base promptings. They are free to roam the whole earth unperceived by you, and by the weight of their numbers bring further and worse, infinitely worse, disasters upon the people of earth.

Why have the Churches so failed to give to the world

the spiritual truth that all these ghastly cataclysms shall be forever banished from off the face of the earth? It is because they know not the truth, and what is so heartrending to us here, they do not *want* to know it.

Those in authority upon earth found at least one of their civil laws upon a dreadful misconception of the nature of 'the life after death'. We in the spirit world have had to stand by helpless while a combination of international authorities commits a fatal blunder. What does it matter, these people say in effect, so long as these detestable criminals are off the earth altogether, where they will never trouble us more? Death is the supreme penalty, the worst punishment that could be meted out to such sub-human creatures who cared nothing for the sanctity of human life. Therefore, let it be death for them. God will deal with them as we never could do. God will show them no mercy, but they will be doomed to spend eternity in Hell, their only sure and right destination.

What folly to suppose that they have been comfortably and tidily *and finally* disposed of, because their lives have been quickly terminated under judicial sentence. Had the earth known one tithe of spiritual truths, wars would have ceased long ere this, but mankind adds one false step to another, and commits this latest culminating blunder.

It is not my purpose, I would ask you to understand, to appear as an 'alarmist' nor is it my intention to exaggerate the present or future case. My friends of old will, I am persuaded, know me better than that I should attempt so doing. What I am trying to do is to show you how, for years, the earth as a whole has existed in a state of spiritual ignorance, with the resulting chaos.

Religion, properly so-called, is not a matter of Church buildings and pleasant, picturesque services, with lights and ornaments, and organs and choirs: something to be thought about upon a Sunday, and little heeded for the rest of the week, except by the professional religionists, the clergy.

True religion is not a matter of pious exercises and grandiloquent prayers spoken in a false, affected voice, and containing little that is of practical spiritual value. Organised religion should know the truth about two worlds, the earth world and the spirit world. Instead, it utters mild rebukes, and tolerates what is patently wrong. It teaches and preaches a tissue of spiritual errors so far removed from the truth as to be fantastic and ludicrous.

The Church has tried to suppress the light wherever it shone forth as a gleam of truth, and preferred to go upon its old way steeped in error. Is it any wonder that the earth, with the Church's teaching to go upon, has done things and said things which in due time have led to terrestrial disasters?

When certain evil men were about to be ejected from the earth, did the Church loudly proclaim that such a course was strictly against that commandment which stands *fifth* upon the list? It preferred to maintain a rigid silence and complete aloofness. If that is God's commandment, there can be no argument about it. The Church, *with one voice*, should have condemned the breaking of it in this and in all cases. The Church has many voices—all different.

Is it supposed that all of the wicked men, or even a substantial proportion of them, who have come to these lands have, upon their dissolution, 'turned over a new leaf', and while in no sense becoming angels, at least shown some signs of repentance?

It would be the height of foolishness to think so. The very nature of their passing has in *so many instances* served to intensify their hatred, and now their aim is to seek vengeance wherever and whenever it is possible. The leaders are here in the spirit world, *a fine concentration of evil.*

Perhaps someone will ask: Why does not God prevent it? The answer is: for the same reason that He did not prevent the outbreak of war in the first instance. Man commits his egregious blunders, and calls upon God to clear them up. The Church prays for guidance, and provides no channels whereby it may be given. Is not that the summit of folly and ignorance?

The earth has been—and is—walking in the darkness, proud of its achievements, its material progress, its social advances; proud of its scientific discoveries, and its noble efforts for the welfare of man. Now you cannot walk in the dark for ever without one day colliding with something heavily, and sustaining accident and injury. As the ways become more intricate, so the obstacles and the snares become more frequent and dangerous, and the casualties increase in numbers. Finally, a fatal tragedy occurs. So has the earth been moving all these years. For this last conflagration, if I may so term it, the inflammable material has been accumulating for long years. In the end it wanted but a spark to fire it, and the spark came.

There is a phrase that has been constantly brought to your notice in the past in connection with your domestic services. It has been treated with derision by some, but all, or a large number of you, have suffered beneath that which the phrase connoted. And that phrase is: *shedding the load.*

That is what the earth has done. It has shed the load of evil on to us in the spirit world for not only have you sent us the evil men themselves, but we in these lands will have to help to put matters right with you.

What right has the earth to evade its responsibilities and cast them upon the shoulders of the people of the spirit world? Upon what divine law is the procedure founded that whenever an individual commits a particular offence he shall be ejected from the earth into spirit lands? Would not the whole earth be horrified if, supposing such a thing were even remotely possible, we returned every single person to the earth whom we, of the spirit world, deemed undesirable to live in these lands?

We could quickly clear the dark realms of its denizens by such direct methods, and so forever abolish the realms of darkness, realms of which we are not the least proud, but in which the earth can have no reason to rejoice for they are solely inhabited by people who once lived upon earth. How would the earth like us to throw back to it all the evil that has been despatched to us here? Yet certain kinds of undesirable citizens are forcibly hurled into these lands in pursuance of certain mundane laws.

Authority on earth fondly believes that by so doing it has, with remarkable cleverness, removed a source of evil from its midst into a place where it can no longer be operative or effective or exert any more influence. What unutterable madness to believe that such is really the case! What stupendous folly! What monumental self-satisfaction! And there is none to say nay to this madness and folly and self-satisfaction but a comparative handful of folk whose voice, though peremptory, is not heeded.

There is not one soul who is in direct communication with us who would not be able to point with unerring precision and exactitude to this as a terrible breach of spiritual law, where, by the decrees of a nation, authority can take it into its own hands to terminate abruptly a man's tenure upon his earthly life.

And so, my friends, by the superior wisdom of the earthly leaders, and by the carrying out of certain judicial sentences, the people of earth are vainly hoping that they have overcome the evil forces on earth at last, whereas, in good truth, what has been done is to cause a concentration of all that evil in the spirit world. Those evil men are *here*, make no mistake about that. They are *alive*, make no mistake about that also. The whole earth is fearful for the future, as well it may be; dreading another and infinitely worse deluge of blood, loss of earthly lives, rending of homes, the destruction and desolation of towns and cities upon a horrifying scale, and the diabolical results and after-results of vast annihilating power. The people of earth have every reason to be frightened.

So—a friendly reader may exclaim to me—you have done a great deal of talking, perhaps you can say what is the remedy for all this? Indeed, yes. It is one of those remedies, simple in themselves, that are so effective if *properly* applied. But the application of the remedy must be done thoroughly, comprehensively, one would say, ruthlessly.

It is this: *the whole earth must undergo a complete and radical change of heart and mind.* And what precisely do I mean by that, you may ask? Just this. Every soul on earth must come to the full realisation of the fact that, throughout the brief period of his life on earth, his duty is to his neighbour, as his neighbour's duty is to him. As an ancient writer has expressed it: do to none other, but that ye would were done to you.

The native of a country thinks of everyone outside his own land as a foreigner. That is wrong. There are no foreigners in the spirit world. We may have belonged to any nation upon earth: here we belong to one land, the huge world of the spirit.

Why should your infinitely *smaller* world divide itself into these narrow 'watertight compartments' of nationality?

The earth has thought that, in the main, it has done nicely for itself, whereas it has blundered and blundered, erected false barriers and distinctions in its social life, and through contentious religious organisations has disseminated spiritual falsity among its people. If the earth desires peace, it must make a fresh start by learning the spiritual truth, and that must be done in the high places wherein are vested the governments of the nations.

Man must know that though the spirit world and the earth world are two separated bodies, yet are they interrelated, and *closely so*. He must realise that we of the spirit world *can and do* communicate with our friends on earth, and that even as we communicate, so can the great ones, the mighty ones, of the highest spheres of spiritual existence also communicate, and from their own great treasury disburse rich stores of knowledge and wisdom. These exalted beings are ready and eager to help the leaders of the earth in all their difficulties and trials, so that by the application of proper and adequate measures eternal peace and prosperity can be brought to the weary earth, with security for the future for all time.

But how is the change of heart and mind to be brought about when the leaders of the nations are spiritually blind? There is too much selfishness upon earth, my friends, and not nearly enough *selflessness*. A change of heart is revolutionary, but only such revolutionary methods will save the earth from future calamity.

Wars increase in violence, intensity, and proportions with each fresh outbreak; they do not diminish in their powers of inflicting devastation, desolation and ruin. There must come a time when a 'saturation point' is reached. Many on earth have expressed the opinion that that time has already arrived. Upon the outset of the next war, they affirm, the world will be annihilated by the stupendous power of the new destructive force. If the earth is to survive, they add, something must be done.

Thus is the light beginning to penetrate in the places where it is darkest and most needed—among the leaders of the nations, for it is *they* who bring wars upon earth, whatever the causes or provocations. The congregation of evil men in the spirit world, who have been sent here by the earth, are not now idle or impotent. They are extremely active and powerful. It is for the people of earth to afford them no opportunity or channel for the fructification of their evil intent. While the leaders essay to pursue fugitive plans for peace upon earth, the evil men are doing their utmost to disrupt those plans, to interpose their malevolent powers in every way possible.

And where, it may be asked, are the 'angels of light' during all this? Are they standing idly by, powerless to stem the flow of evil, powerless to effect any good upon earth? No, they are not standing idle, by any means. But whether the people of the spirit world can influence the minds of the earth world's leaders and their underlings rests with both the latter.

We try strenuously to impinge upon their minds the right course to take. Some may hear us, and be thoroughly convinced that the thoughts that have 'come into their heads' are the only sound and safe and sure solution of some particular problem. What happens? Such folk are a minority; one voice, perhaps, crying in the wilderness and what a wilderness! It may be heard—there are true prophets upon earth—but most assuredly it will not be heeded. There are other influences at work, theories to be tested, interests to be protected and served at all costs, money to be thought of, petty rules and tortuous modes of procedure to be observed, and prejudice, pride, and pure idiocy to cause obstructions.

Indeed, no; the people of the spirit world will never abandon their brothers upon earth, whose need is more imperative now than ever it has been throughout the course of time and history. If only man would heed the voices from these exalted realms of the spirit of which I have spoken. It makes us weep to see the earth slipping deeper and ever deeper into the morass of world disorder.

Great days of national prayer, my friends, are of little or no avail. What is being prayed for, would you say? Guidance, perhaps? Just so. If the guidance is given, what then? Will any attention be paid to it? *That guidance has already been given* without reference to any impressive assemblies of important personages in a grand display of religious fervour. Praying for mercy because the Church pronounces the people of earth to be all 'miserable sinners', and reciting long and most inappropriate prayers, will produce no results whatever. It would be better if these important folk were to meet in their own chamber, and with earnestness in their hearts and with a deep and sincere resolve to act upon their impressions utterly regardless of preconceptions or prejudices, and to pray: 'Great Father, through your ministers of light show us what to do, and whatsoever it may be, that we promise to do unfailingly.'

That, my dear friends, would produce far grander results than all the exaggerated solemnity of any 'calls to prayer'—and such prayer, too. Does the Father of the Universe like His children to cringe to Him? Would you, my friends, who have children of your own to whom you are devoted, would you like them to cringe to you? Of course not. You would be revolted by the spectacle and wonder what was amiss with them—or with yourself— that they should so behave.

Then, would I say to you, be forthright in manly and womanly fashion, and in simple unaffected terms, such as you would employ amongst yourselves in your own homestead, address the Father of us all, and ask Him to help your old earth out of its deep troubles and miseries. We shall unite in all efforts that are truly directed towards that one goal of peace on earth to men of good will. For *true* peace is not a matter of signatures upon documents. With u*niversal good will* peace is in sight.

The earth has already vanquished the forces of evil with the untiring and ungrudging help of its unseen friends of the spirit world, but the earth, by its present blunders, has shifted the power of evil from its own world into ours. It has banished the evil in physical form, but it still remains active in spirit form, having gathered more force in its wicked career. Help us, then, to help you, to prevent any further irruption of evil upon earth. Those evil forces cannot hurt us in these and other realms of light, but they can hurt you, hurt you dreadfully, and again bring abomination and desolation upon the earth.

And now, my friends, the time has come for me to close these present writings. We have covered a little ground together, and I hope the journey we have taken thus has not been tedious to you. If there are things we have not discussed, it is because space, though unlimited in the spirit realms, is very much limited when we visit the earth and speak through the medium of words [to be] printed on paper! We must therefore cut our coat according to our cloth.

That tranquillity and prosperity will again be your pleasure is the profound wish of us all in these lands, and with God's help, through His able, though unseen ministers, both will be restored to you. And in all your strivings towards that happy end, I would say:

Benedicat te omnipotens Deus

9 781908 421432